T0340347

Computable General Equilibrium Modeling

Many books have been written on computable general equilibrium (CGE) modeling. However, there are certain important areas for economic policy that have been largely overlooked. This intermediate/advanced text presents the topic as a methodology for the analysis of macro and fiscal policies in modern economies while introducing levels of disaggregation that are beyond the scope of standard macro models.

The book begins by presenting the historical and intuitive background of general equilibrium analysis. Moving on, computer software is introduced to derive numerical solutions for economic models. The authors provide examples of code, bringing in data sources that have become the foundations of CGE applications. The methodology presented here, which differs from other CGE books, includes financial assets, government budget deficits, and debt financing of private investment. These topics are analyzed in the context of dynamic optimization, generating endogenous variables such as inflation, interest, and growth rates. The book also devotes significant attention to the applications of CGE models to developing economies.

This textbook comes with a range of downloadable supplements and will be a valuable resource for students taking a CGE course as part of a program in advanced microeconomics, macroeconomics, development economics, or international trade economics.

Kenneth Castellanos is Associate Analyst at the Congressional Budget Office, USA.

Andrew Feltenstein is Professor of Economics, Emeritus, at Georgia State University, USA.

Gohar Sedrakyan is Clinical Assistant Professor of Economics and Affiliated Scholar at Kennesaw State University, USA.

"A very clearly written and self-contained guide to applying state-of-the-art computable general equilibrium models to key issues in modern macroeconomics. The applications to developing economies are particularly compelling, including how to incorporate the underground economy and financial repression. An important reference for students, researchers, and practitioners."

Kenneth Rogoff, *Maurits C. Boas Professor of Economics, Harvard University, https://scholar.harvard.edu/rogoff*

"Computable General Equilibrium (CGE) modelling is an essential tool in economics. This book by a team led by one of the most eminent international scholars in CGE modelling will become the go-to for teaching this subject. Generally, students, researchers and practitioners will profit from the insights in this excellent volume."

Jorge Martinez-Vazquez, *Founding Director International Center for Public Policy, Georgia State University*

"This book provides a detailed and useful introduction for students of economics to CGE models. The book extends their applications to include areas such as monetary theory, tax evasion, development economics and others, areas that have become relevant in today's environment."

Vito Tanzi, *PhD, Honorary President, International Institute of Public Finance*

Computable General Equilibrium Modeling

Theory and Applications

Kenneth Castellanos, Andrew Feltenstein and Gohar Sedrakyan

LONDON AND NEW YORK

Designed cover image: © aluxum/Getty Images

First published 2024
by Routledge
4 Park Square, Milton Park, Abingdon, Oxon OX14 4RN

and by Routledge
605 Third Avenue, New York, NY 10158

Routledge is an imprint of the Taylor & Francis Group, an informa business

© 2024 Kenneth Castellanos, Andrew Feltenstein and Gohar Sedrakyan

The right of Kenneth Castellanos, Andrew Feltenstein and Gohar Sedrakyan to be identified as authors of this work has been asserted in accordance with sections 77 and 78 of the Copyright, Designs and Patents Act 1988.

The views expressed in this book are the authors' and should not be interpreted as CBO's.

British Library Cataloguing-in-Publication Data
A catalogue record for this book is available from the British Library

Library of Congress Cataloging-in-Publication Data
Names: Castellanos, Kenneth, author. | Feltenstein, Andrew, author. |
    Sedrakyan, Gohar, author.
Title: Computable general equilibrium modeling : theory and applications /
    Kenneth Castellanos, Andrew Feltenstein and Gohar Sedrakyan.
Description: 1 Edition. | New York, NY : Routledge, 2024. | Includes
    bibliographical references and index.
Identifiers: LCCN 2023014564 | ISBN 9780367272074 (hardback) |
    ISBN 9780367272050 (paperback) | ISBN 9780429295485 (ebook)
Subjects: LCSH: Computable general equilibrium models.
Classification: LCC HB141.3.C66 C37 2024 | DDC 330.01/5195—dc23/
    eng/20230605
LC record available at https://lccn.loc.gov/2023014564

ISBN: 978-0-367-27207-4 (hbk)
ISBN: 978-0-367-27205-0 (pbk)
ISBN: 978-0-429-29548-5 (ebk)

DOI: 10.4324/9780429295485

Typeset in Times New Roman
by Apex CoVantage, LLC

Access the Support Material: www.routledge.com/9780367272050

Contents

Preface

Many books have been written on CGE modeling.[1] However, there are certain important areas for economic policy that have been largely overlooked. Textbooks typically have not looked at macroeconomic applications of CGE techniques. Thus, for example, there is usually little or no analysis of the implications of deficit financing since the models developed in these books generally do not incorporate financial assets and hence cannot address mechanisms, such as borrowing or monetization, that are generally used to finance deficits. Also, the interest rate impact of government borrowing on savings and investment cannot be dealt with directly. In short, standard CGE methodology, as presented in most textbooks, leaves out many of the key issues and instruments in public policy. The essential aim of this book is thus to show how CGE modeling can analyze a broad range of issues that are important for public policy while at the same time being able to maintain degrees of disaggregation in production and consumption that are beyond the scope of standard macro models.

The book will also introduce a number of important policy and technical issues that are not normally included in CGE books. For example, a major topic in public finance is the analysis of tax evasion and its implications for the economy. See Tanzi (2001) for a discussion of the importance of this issue. We will show how tax evasion can be introduced into the CGE model as a form of optimizing behavior so that we will see how agents' compliance varies with tax rates and other parameters in the economy. The book also looks at financial constraints to development, in particular credit rationing by banks as well as international constraints on public borrowing, which have differing impacts on different sectors of the economy. These issues are difficult to analyze in the context of standard macro models since they generally cannot examine disaggregated consumption or production. Typical static, real sector CGE models also cannot look at these problems since they do not incorporate financial assets or time dimensions.

The book first discusses, in a broad, nontechnical context, the theoretical background of general equilibrium analysis, the Arrow-Debreu model (Debreu, 1959). We will then outline the algorithm that solves Kakutani's fixed point theorem, which is the basis for the solution method we use to solve general equilibrium systems. As the book progresses, computer software will be introduced to derive numerical solutions for the sorts of economic models we are developing at that stage. We simultaneously introduce the sort of data sources that have become the building blocks of CGE applications. Thus, we will cover the use of social accounting matrices (SAM) and input-output matrices as building blocks that can be used to simplify the construction of CGE models as well as to reduce the computational burden of the models.

We will then show how our computational techniques can be used to analyze public policies in the context of a dynamic framework with considerable macroeconomic content. The methodology will thus differ from that normally presented in CGE books in that we will incorporate financial assets, government budget deficits, and debt financing of private investment that competes with public debt. The student using the book will thus be familiar with techniques that can be very useful in real-world applications. The book will also devote several sections to looking at applications of CGE models to developing countries, a common topic of study in international agencies such as the World Bank and International Monetary Fund. Our macro-based approach will be especially useful here.

Note

1 See, for example, Burfisher (2001), Cardenete et al. (2017), Chang (2022), Dixon and Jorgenson (2012), and Ginsburgh and Keyzer (1997).

1 Introduction

1.1 Historical background

Economists have had the general idea of a market equilibrium since the very beginning of the study of economics. More specifically, the definition of an equilibrium being a set of prices at which markets clear is evident in Adam Smith (1776), in the famous story of the customer and the baker. Here the customer goes to the baker to buy a loaf of bread. He purchases exactly the amount of bread he desires, maximizing his utility function, at the market price of bread. The baker maximizes his profits by selling bread at this market price and sells the customer exactly the quantity of bread that he demands. The customer and the baker do not know each other, and they only interact through the price system. Nonetheless, they both go away happy. This interaction is repeated across many bakers and many customers, and the overall market for bread clears. There is just one question: what is the market clearing price for bread? Our intuition tells us that if it is too low, then the customers will demand too much, and the profit-maximizing bakers will produce too little. Hence there will be excess demand. Conversely, if the price is too high, then bakers will produce too much, and consumers will demand too little, leading to excess supply. How is the correct "market clearing" price to be determined?

If we look at the broader macro economy, we need a set of prices that clear all markets so that supply equals demand in the markets for butchers, bakers, and candlestick makers. There are really two essential questions. The first question is whether such a set of prices exist. The second question is just how the market achieves these prices. That is, without a central planner to set prices, what sort of market mechanism causes price adjustments to occur so that all markets clear? What might one's intuition be? There is often a vague notion that if there is excess demand in a market, then the price will rise, and if there is excess supply, then the price will fall. Early economists thus believed that such a price adjustment mechanism would eventually lead to an equilibrium.

Another, more mathematical approach came from a group of European economists, such as Léon Walras (1954) and Michael Barone. These and other economists thought of markets in terms of excess demand equations with one equation for each good. Hence, for example, excess demand for apples is expressed by a single equation, in which excess demand depends upon all prices simultaneously.

DOI: 10.4324/9780429295485-1

Since each excess demand equation depends upon all prices, then if there are N prices, then there are N excess demand equations in N unknowns. Accordingly, they thought that the solution for a competitive equilibrium consisted in solving N equations in N unknowns. It was known that the solution to such a problem exists, even though that solution might be difficult to derive.

However, they failed to realize that there is no guarantee that the solution to these N equations will necessarily be N positive numbers, the only outcome that makes economic sense. Thus, for example, the solution could include negative numbers for some prices and imaginary numbers for other prices. Of course, such numbers are meaningless from an economic point of view. There would need to be some attribute to the system of supply and demand equations that would guarantee a solution with all positive (or zero) numbers and no negative or imaginary numbers. What these attributes need to be was totally unknown. At the same time, there was no mathematical solution to the issue of how the economy would move to an equilibrium. If, for example, something in the economy changes, say, a new tax regime, then how will prices adjust to arrive at a new market equilibrium of no excess demand?

Additionally, these nineteenth-century economists seem to have had a belief that you could go from an individual's maximization problems to a single problem for the economy as a whole. That is, the individual's problem is the following:

$$Max\, U(x)\, s.t.$$

$$\sum_{i=1}^{N} p_i x_i \leq p_i r_i$$

$$\rightarrow \sum_{i=1}^{N} p_i (x_i - r_i) \leq 0$$

If we aggregate over all consumers, this becomes Walras' law; the aggregate value of excess demand is 0.

Why can't we turn the individual's maximization problem into a global central planning problem? That is, max $GNP\, s.t.\, prices = \vec{p}$, where $\vec{p}$ has been chosen to maximize GNP. Intuitively, there are two problems with this approach. The first problem is that a random set of prices will not be consistent with market clearing. That is, if prices are arbitrarily changed so as to increase GNP, we will not realize supply equals demand in all markets. The second problem is that there is no clearly defined market mechanism that would generate prices that maximize GNP. Accordingly, there were many attempts to reframe the equilibrium problem as a central planner's adjustment mechanism.

One of the best known such approach was due to Oskar Lange (1967). He starts by letting the State have partial ownership of all scarce resources. That is, the state owns the capital stock but has only limited control over labor. The State would then allocate capital according to its scarcity value in different industries. Suppose that the state's objective function remains the maximization of GDP. Then if the state determines the need for reallocating capital from one sector of the economy to another, then it will do so as part of its overall central plan. This approach does not formally introduce the role of consumers. Rather, the objective function is to achieve the targets of the central plan with the most efficient use of factor inputs. Presumably the central government would then allocate final goods according to some social planning mechanism. Apart from difficulties in implementation, such an approach would be clearly unacceptable in the modern context.

Apart from the ideological issues of this central planning approach, there is no explanation of how this efficient allocation of factors would be determined. In general, the view was that the problem, although large, simply amounted to solving multiple equations in multiple unknowns. The free market opponents to this central planning worldview, Friedrich Hayek (1935, 1940) and Lionel Robbins (1937), for example, said that even if all the ownership of resources was given to the State, there would still be too many equations to solve in those pre-computer days. Thus, the central planning approach to equilibrium could never be practically implemented.

Lange (1967), a socialist, believed that the problem of many equations and prices could be overcome by using a tatonnement procedure. This is often referred to as a method of steepest ascent, in which prices adjust to mimic the behavior of a market and thereby supposedly will eventually achieve a market equilibrium.

1.2 Intuition of computation

What is tatonnement? Suppose that there is a market mechanism, what Léon Walras referred to as the invisible hand of the marketplace, that adjusts prices according to excess demand for products. The adjustment mechanism is as follows:

$$p_i' = p_i + \delta_i g_i(p)\, where:$$

$$\delta_i \geq 0 \ and \ g_i(p) = excess\ demand\ for\ good\ i$$

Here δ_i is the speed of adjustment to excess demand in the ith market. The problem about this method (unknown to Lange) is that it is not globally stable. That is, depending upon where the process starts, it may never converge. This is not only an issue for computer programmers but also for real-world simulation exercises. Thus, suppose that a hypothetical economy is at an equilibrium and the government then changes tax rates. Presumably the economy will seek a new equilibrium, but if we use the old equilibrium as a starting point and then try to move to the new equilibrium via the tatonnement process, the process may not work. Thus, this attempt to have central planning mimic a market mechanism might fail.

A much later result is that the tatonnement methodology can be proven to converge only if excess demands for all goods are gross substitutes. This essentially means that if the price for one good rises, then demand for all other goods rises. This almost never happens, so this apparently intuitive approach is found to be uncertain.

So how are we to reach an equilibrium? Consider the N dimensional price simplex. That is as follows:

$$\{p_i\} \, s.t. \sum_{i=1}^{N} p_i = 1$$

If we restrict ourselves to economies that are homogeneous of degree 0, then we could look for an equilibrium on the simplex. Homogeneity of degree 0 means that if all prices are multiplied by a constant, then there is no change in demand or supply. In macro terms, this means no money illusion. Would a random search on the simplex lead to an equilibrium? Short answer is no, so what should be done? The first big breakthroughs came from researchers who were not really economists.

Carlton Lemke, an applied mathematician at the Rensselaer Polytechnic Institute, was working on solutions to two-person non-zero-sum games. He came up with an algorithm that took discrete steps, did not depend upon or use differentiability, and ended in a finite number of steps. This approach was a breakthrough in several ways. First, it led people away from the notion that they must depend upon continuity (and hence calculus) in finding an equilibrium. Second, it led researchers away from asymptotic methods which only stop when the computer tells them to stop; rather the search will stop on its own in a finite number of steps (Lemke and Howson, 1964).

Then there were a series of advancements in the general theory. Harold Kuhn (Princeton) used a theorem in mathematics, Kakutani's fixed point theorem, to extend Lemke's approach. This was an especially important innovation, as the use of this fixed-point theorem became the basis of a large part of applied general equilibrium analysis (Kuhn, 1960). Still, however, the profession had not realized the connection between solving these game theory problems, fixed point theorems, and the solution to the economic problem of a competitive equilibrium. The major breakthrough came in 1967 and was made by Herbert Scarf at Yale University. Scarf made the mechanical connection between the solution to non-zero-sum games and the general equilibrium model (Scarf, 1967a, 1967b).

1.3   Areas of application

The Scarf approach was, initially, only applied to pure production and consumption economies. That is, to economies that do not have taxes, public spending, or any government at all. Expanding the economy to include a government adds a number of complexities that we will discuss in later chapters. For now, let us just say that the key innovations that permit the applied general equilibrium model to include a public sector were made by John Shoven and John Whalley (1973), who began their work while graduate students at Yale University. They developed an approach that expands the dimensions of the general equilibrium model and thereby permits the incorporation of, in particular, taxes. Shoven and Whalley thus introduced taxes using an approach based upon the algorithm developed by Scarf that iteratively arrives at prices for which supply equals demand for all goods, factors, and financial assets. The only conditions needed for the methodology to work successfully are that the supply and demand functions be continuous, homogenous of degree 0, and satisfy Walras' law. See Kehoe and Kehoe (1995) for a description of the general static model with an application to the US.

The Shoven and Whalley (1973) introduction of taxes into the computable general equilibrium model immediately opened the path to a wide variety of possible policy applications. Among such applications are all forms of taxation, including indirect, direct, and property. If taxes represent government collections of revenues from the public, the reverse are subsidies which transfer revenues from the government to the public. Thus, the CGE models are also used to study the implications of various forms of government subsidies (Fehr et al., 1995; Fossati and Wiegard, 2002; Perali and Scandizzo, 2018). Further, the studies of taxes and other regulations (e.g., local content requirements) on the bilateral flow of international trade make use of CGE models (Park, 1995; Gilbert et al., 2010; Eromenko, 2011; Das and Chakraborti, 2014; Dixon et al., 2018; Feltenstein and Plassmann, 2008; Harrison et al., 1997). Recent work, such as Bovenberg and Goulder (1996), Castellanos (2021), and Castellanos and Heutel (2019), examines the role of environmental taxes.

Later studies found the CGE models equally beneficial in applying them to the other side of the government's balance sheet and using them in investigation of broad areas of government expenditures and topics of reducing public debt. See, for example, Auerbach and Kotlikoff (1987) with an application to social security, among other topics. The determination of the optimizing behavior of a central bank also found its explanations through the CGE models (Taylor, 1990; Breisinger, 2006; Hosoe et al., 2010; Amir, 2012). In recent years, with new economic challenges, despite the vast available methodologies to study those arising topics, the CGE models have found increasingly wider use in these areas. Some of those contemporary topics include, but are not limited to, environmental economics, tourism, production and supply challenges (e.g., food), regional economics and gender inclusivity (Doi, 2003; Do, 2009; André et al., 2010; Abrell, 2011; Tanaka et al., 2012; Barun Deb Pal et al., 2015; Meng and Siriwardana, 2017; Mohammed and Jabin, 2019; Kabir and Dudu, 2020; Madden et al., 2020). The next chapter explores some of these topics in greater detail and outlines the CGE framework and tools that this textbook offers to analyze them.

2 Applications

This book discusses the general framework of computational general equilibrium (CGE) models, which can be applied to a wide spectrum of questions in public policies. Thus, the Shoven and Whalley model (1973) introduced taxes into CGE model, which paved the way for an abundance of possible public policy applications. Among such applications are the following:

2.1 Indirect taxes

Indirect taxes may briefly be described as ad valorem taxes upon the purchase or sales of final, intermediate, or primary goods.[1] Among such taxes, which will be discussed in depth later in the book, are the following:

2.1.1 Sales taxes

Sales taxes are used widely at the state level in the United States. They are generally leveled on the purchase of a final good or service (for example, a shirt or a haircut) and are paid by the consumer who makes the purchase. From the point of view of the general equilibrium economist, these taxes are immediately interesting since they change the structure of relative prices in the economy.

2.1.2 Value-Added Taxes (VAT)

This type of taxes is quite rare in the USA but is widely used in the rest of the world. Here taxes are levied on the value added at each stage of production. That is, the value of inputs of scarce factors, such as capital and labor, are taxed as the production process goes forward. The final purchaser then only pays the tax on the value added at the final stage of the production process. Thus, for example, when a consumer purchases a shirt at a retail store, he pays taxes only on the value added at the final stage of the production process, that is, the retail store. The underlying idea for VAT is that they avoid a "cascading" of effective tax rates. See Bye et al. (2003) for a discussion of VAT in a similar context to that discussed here.

DOI: 10.4324/9780429295485-2

2.1.3 *Tariffs on imports, customs duties, and quotas*

An *import tariff* is mechanically similar to a sales tax. A foreign commodity enters the country, and a tax on the imported value of that commodity is paid by the purchaser. This tax is thus based upon the foreign value of the good, the exchange rate, and any possible markup by the importer.

Customs duty is another fee on imported products which arises when a good is transported across international border and is usually collected at the border. The payor of the fee is the individual or entity importing that good. The government regulations may assign a duty-free amount, which is exempt from the payment. Any amount exceeding the legally mandated minimum level will require the payment of customs duty. For instance, an individual returning to the US from Europe with two liters of alcohol will use the exemption on one liter and pay customs duty on the remaining one liter of imported alcoholic beverage. Customs duties are important for policy analysis since they are used as instruments of trade protection. Since they often protect noncompetitive domestic industries, they can be highly distortionary.

The government may impose *limits (quotas) on the quantity or the value of goods* allowed to be imported to the country. There is no extra tax revenue directly collected by the government, per se, but the use of this policy tool may generate stimulus for the domestic producers and may result in higher prices passed on the domestic consumers.

2.1.4 *Export taxes*

These are relatively unusual; however, they have been used by some countries. Typically, the country is an exporter of a primary good, for which demand is believed to be relatively inelastic. The country then taxes the exporter (who is often the producer and may well be a state-owned enterprise). The tax is then passed on in the form of a higher price to the eventual foreign importer.

2.2 Direct taxes

These are taxes that, unlike indirect taxes, are not levied upon specific transactions, such as purchases of goods or services, but are levied upon income flows. Among such taxes are the following:

2.2.1 *Personal income tax*

These taxes are practically universal. An individual receives income from a variety of sources, such as wages, rental income, investment income, entrepreneurial income, and other sources. Then the levied tax bill is based upon many factors such as the level and source of received income. Most countries have some version of a progressive income tax in which tax rates rise as the taxpayer's income rises.

2.2.2 *Corporate income tax*

This is also an almost universally applied tax that is levied upon corporate profits. The interpretation of the tax is that it is applied to returns to capital and thus bears relatively more heavily upon capital intensive sectors of the economy. An example of such an application the USA is given in Fullerton et al. (1981).

2.2.3 *Wealth tax*

Unlike the personal and corporate income taxes that are levied upon income flows, the wealth tax is applied to the assessed value of an individual's personal wealth, which may be derived from a variety of assets. Thus, for example, a picture on the wall has an assessed value and part of a person's wealth, and hence may be taxed under a wealth tax. Since there is no corresponding income flow, such a tax may generate interesting general equilibrium effects. For example, the wealth holder may sell the asset in order to pay the tax.

2.2.4 *Land and property taxes*

Land and property taxes are a type of wealth tax in that they are levied upon the assessed value of a parcel of land or a property (house, apartment, collection of art, etc.), and there is no corresponding income flow. From the point of view of general equilibrium analysis, the fact that land and property values vary by location leads to issues of mobility when land or property is taxed. That is, might a landholder move to a less expensive area to avoid or reduce the land tax? Unlike almost all other taxed assets, land is completely immobile so that there are no means, in general, to reduce the arising tax liability other than by selling the land. A painting, on the other hand, could always be moved to a different tax jurisdiction.

2.3 Subsidies

Taxes represent government collections of revenues from the public. In contrast, subsidies are transfers of revenues from the government to the public. Like taxes, subsidies can have strong general equilibrium effects in changing individual incomes as well as relative prices. Subsidies are, in many countries, major parts of government budgets and have significant impacts upon the macro economy. The CGE modeling approach is found to be very useful in the analysis of such effects. Among the general types of subsidies are the following.

2.3.1 *Price supports*

These are policies to support the domestic price of a product. Suppose, for example, that the world price of a domestically manufactured product has fallen. In this case the government might want to keep high prices for the domestic producers, so as to, possibly, keep them in business, while at the same time pass on the low prices to consumers. The government could do so by paying a subsidy, equal to the difference between the consumers' price and the producers' price. This subsidy would thus look like a negative sales tax, in that consumers pay less but producers receive more. Such price-support subsidies are very expensive for governments, as the low consumer prices increase demand, and hence increase the portion of government payments to producers.

2.3.2 *Lump sum transfers*

Governments make a wide variety of lump sum transfer payments. Thus, for example, food stamps and unemployment benefits are typical examples. As with price supports, lump sum transfers will impact the government budget, change relative prices, and affect consumption patterns. Lump sum transfers are often proposed as being more efficient than price supports, in that it is possible to use them to target a specific population. Thus, for example, rather than subsidize the price of fuel, one might give lump sum transfers to low-income groups, so that high-income groups would not benefit from cheap gasoline.

2.4   Government spending

Although computational general equilibrium (CGE) modeling initially focused on tax policies, the other side of the government's balance sheet is equally important. The following broad areas of expenditures are being considered.

2.4.1 *Current spending*

Current spending includes all spending on goods and services. This would thus include social programs such as social security, public pension plans, and welfare. Other expenditures such as defense, environmental programs, education, and many other programs that constitute a large part of public outlays would also be included in public spending. See, for example, Tanzi (2001), and Tanzi and Schuknecht (2000) for a discussion of this topic. These programs impact private sector output and consumption and relative prices. Here, the dynamics of economic growth are a major focus of applied general equilibrium analysis.

2.4.2 *Capital expenditure with implications for the private sector*

Capital expenditure represents a major portion of government budgets around the world. The general objective of capital expenditure is to enhance the productivity of the economy, in particular of the private sector. Applied general equilibrium models offer a well-defined methodology to analyze the implications of such spending. For example, what is the trade-off between increased public debt and resulting higher interest rate and reduced marginal costs of production caused by improved public infrastructure?

2.5   Financing budget deficits

Once taxation and public spending are introduced, the next related topic is to consider how to deal with budget deficits. This closely links to the topic of how deficits are financed. That is, they require the introduction of financial assets, government bonds, and money. Many CGE models, up to today, have avoided financial assets, because to handle them in a structurally correct way requires the use of dynamic models. That is, it makes little sense to introduce borrowing with interest repayment in a static model. Of course, having a time dimension requires agents that carry out dynamic optimization, which makes the model more complex. Nonetheless, we will introduce a method for incorporating budget deficits and financial assets in the CGE model and will thereby enhance the scope of our analysis.

2.5.1   Mix of borrowing and monetization

One of key policy decisions carried out by governments is determining the mix of budget deficit financing by debt and monetization. We will be able to incorporate the exogenous, policy determined ratios of debt and money debt financing, and generate the general equilibrium outcomes resulting from those policy decisions.

2.5.2   Foreign borrowing

Countries may choose to draw on domestic or foreign resources in order to finance their borrowing needs. We will be able to introduce foreign currency into our model, and in doing so open the possibility of foreign borrowing based upon the equilibrium between the foreign supply of financial assets and the domestic demand for those foreign assets. Additionally, we may introduce fixed and floating exchange rates as policy instruments.

The domestic resources may also rise due to the advantageous position of countries to attract foreign capital in the form of foreign direct investments (FDI). In general, business investments in a foreign country are considered to be a risky type of asset allocation; consequently, the destination countries which raise this source of foreign capital are comparatively limited. The studies on foreign direct investments, to certain extent, resemble the analysis associated with some of the topics in international trade and, as such, are of the interest to practitioners who use CGE models.

2.6   Central bank behavior

We will continue and add macroeconomic elements to our CGE approach. Among such elements are issues concerning the optimizing behavior of a central bank, which will be a type of economic agent in the model. Among these operational issues are open market operations, reserve requirements, discount lending to the private banking system, and interest rate targeting. Bringing the central bank into our model is important since the interaction between the bank and the treasury, through the financing of the public budget deficit, will reverberate through the entire economy.

2.7 Foreign sector

Incorporating a foreign sector allows us to continue to enhance the realism and empirical content of our CGE model. There are various empirical and theoretical building blocks to the construction of a foreign sector. The use of specific country examples will help estimate and incorporate the following methods and factors:

2.7.1 Export and import equations

We will estimate trade elasticities based upon relative price levels, exchange rates, and world and domestic incomes.

2.7.2 Endogenous capital flows

These will depend upon consumer optimizing behavior, as well as risk parameters to be estimated and incorporated in the models we develop.

i. *Capital flight*
This will be part of the incorporation of endogenous capital flows.

ii. *Exchange rate regimes*
A number of policy objectives will be covered, including the fixed and floating exchange rates, managed floats, and "leaning against the wind" strategy.

iii. Another related topic, *quotas on imports*, will be examined. Here, the CGE methodology will be used to compute the shadow price of a quota, which directly impacts the exchange rate. This shadow price may be interpreted as the amount people would be willing to pay to have the import quota relaxed.

iv. *Some very preliminary model intuition.*
Let's now consider how to solve a very simple pure exchange economy. That is, no production. There are simply a group of agents who trade their initial endowments.
Assume that utility functions are quasi-concave.

$$U\left(\alpha x + \left(1 - \alpha\right)x'\right) \geq \min\left(U\left(x\right), U\left(x'\right)\right)$$

Each consumer has an endowment

$$w = \left(w_1, \ldots, w_N\right)$$

The consumer's income is as follows:

$$I(p) = \sum_{1}^{N} p_i w_i$$

The problem for each consumer is as follows:

$$\max U(x) \, such that \, p \cdot x \le I(p)$$

Homogeneity allows us to assume:

$$\sum p_i = 1$$

$$U(x') \ge \alpha U(x_1) + (1-\alpha) U(x_2)$$

Assume also that:

$$U(\lambda x) = \lambda U(x)$$

Assume also that all consumers have identical utility functions. The *separating hyperplane theorem*[2] says that:

$$\exists p^* s.t. \, p^* w = u(w)$$

$$p^* x \ge u(x)$$

$$p^* = \left\{ \frac{\partial u}{\partial x_i} \right\} \lceil w$$

So we must have the following:

$$u(x) \le p^* \cdot x \le p^* w^i$$

For any x that satisfies the budget constraint. Then

$$p^* w^i = \frac{p^* w^i}{p^* w} \cdot u(w) \, as \, p^* w = u(w) \, so:$$

$$= u\left(\frac{p^* w^i}{p^* w} \cdot w \right) \to d^i(p^*) = \frac{p^* w^i}{p^* w} \cdot w$$

as this maximizes over x satisfying the budget constraint. Also:

$$\sum_i d^i(p^*) = w \sum_i \frac{p^* w^i}{p^* w} = w$$

So we have market clearing.

This result is limited and not of much practical use since it reflects only an exchange economy and hence does not address the real-world issue of production and how it impacts prices and equilibria. It also assumes that all consumers have identical utility functions, which is also clearly unrealistic. Now we will begin turning to steps to solve the more general model.

Notes

1 There are other indirect taxes, which will be discussed in later chapters. Our current focus is only on ad valorem taxes.
2 See, for example, Koopmans (1957).

3   Fixed points

Applied general equilibrium computation, using our approach, depends upon find-ing a "fixed point" to the underlying economy. The idea of a fixed point of a func-tion is simple. Suppose that we have a function $f(x)$ that maps a space S onto itself. That is:

$$f : S \rightarrow S$$

Then a fixed point would be an element from the space S, expressed as $x \in S \, s.t. \, f(x) = x$ if $f(x)$ is a single valued function. For example, suppose our mapping is the single valued function $f(x) = x^2$. Then f has an obvious fixed point, expressed as $x = 1$, since $f(1) = 1^2 = 1$.

What would be an example of a fixed point of a set valued function? Let us take an example from micro economics. Suppose we have a standard utility function $U(x) \, where \, x \, is \, consumption$. We will then define our mapping as being the indif-ference curve. That is:

$$f(x) = \{y\} \, s.t. U(x) = U(y)$$

Then, of course, x lies on its own indifference curve. That is:

$$x \in \{y\} \, as \, U(x) = U(y)$$

Thus, we are defining the projection mapping onto the indifference curve (Figure 3.1).

3.1   Mappings

A "mapping," for our purposes, can be considered to be a set of functions that takes a closed space onto itself. Thus, in the diagram in the next section, the function $f(x)$ takes the point $x \rightarrow f(x)$ (Figure 3.2). Thus, for example, if the space is defined as $S = \{x\} \, s.t. 0 \le x \le 1$, then the function $f(x) = x^2$ maps S onto itself. On the other hand, if we define $S = \{x\} \, s.t. 0 \le x \le 2$, then the same function does *not* map S onto itself, since $2^2 = 4$.

DOI: 10.4324/9780429295485-3

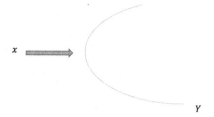

Figure 3.1 Projection mapping onto the indifference curve

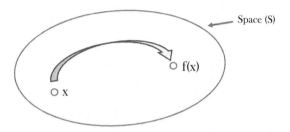

Figure 3.2 Mapping Example 1

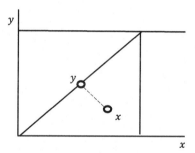

Figure 3.3 Mapping Example 2

Another example of a mapping would be to map the point $x = \{x_1, x_{,2}\} \to y$ where y is the orthogonal projection of x onto the diagonal of the unit square, as shown here (Figure 3.3).

More formally, we would define the mapping here as follows:

$$y_1 = \frac{x_1 + x_2}{2}$$

$$y_2 = \frac{x_1 + x_2}{2}$$

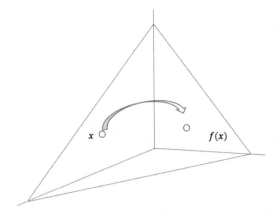

Figure 3.4 Mapping Example 3

Suppose we are now thinking in terms of more than two dimensions and consider the mapping of the unit simplex on to itself. Graphically, the mapping would look like (Figure 3.4).

More formally, this would be a mapping:

$$y_1 = f_1(x)$$

$$\vdots$$

$$y_n = f_n(x)$$

With the following set of conditions:

1) $f_i(x) \geq 0 \, \forall i$

$$\sum_{i=1}^{N} f_i(x) = 1$$

2) $f_i(x)$ *is continuous*

Let us consider a simple example of an exchange economy.

Example

An exchange economy consists only of consumers who trade their endowments of goods. There is no production and no businesses. Suppose that the initial endowments are not in equilibrium in the sense that demand and supply are not equal for at least some goods. Therefore, the task is to find an equilibrium set of prices such that supply equals demand when all consumers are maximizing at those prices. Suppose we start at an arbitrary price vector p. An intuitively attractive way to begin might be to simply look at excess demand for each good at the price vector p. Then there will be an increase in the prices $\{p_i\}$ for which there is excess demand, and a decrease in those prices for which there is excess supply. The largest increases (decreases) will be made for those prices where the excess demand (supply) is greatest. Such an approach is typically called the *method of steepest ascent*.

Suppose the method of steepest ascent is used. Let

$$g_i(p) = i^{th} \text{ excess demand}$$

According to Walras' law, the value of aggregate excess demand must be 0. This is the circularity of income. That is:

$$\sum p_i g_i(p) = 0$$

Next, to define a mapping from the price simplex onto something else:

$$p_i \to p_i + g_i(p)$$

Since $g_i(p)$, excess demand for the ith good at prices p can have any value, positive or negative, then the mapping does not necessarily lie on the unit simplex. Thus, to define a new mapping p_i' where:

$$p_i' = \frac{p_i + \max(0, g_i(p))}{1 + \sum max(0, g_i(p))} \tag{1}$$

In other words, p_i' is estimated as the ratio of the highest of 0 and excess demand $(g_i(p))$ added to the price level (p_i) of that individual good and divided by summation of all maximization decisions plus 1.

We then have:

$$\sum_i p_i' = \sum_i \left\{ \frac{p_i + max(0, g_i(p))}{1 + \sum max(0, g_i(p))} \right\} = 1$$

This new mapping does indeed lie on the simplex.

3.2   Brouwer fixed point theorem[1]

Brouwer fixed point theorem is key to general equilibrium theory as well as to CGE modeling. The theorem states the following:

Suppose that f is a continuous function that takes the simplex onto itself. Then:

$$\exists x^* \text{ s.t. } f(x^*) = x^*$$

That is, there is some point x^* which is mapped onto itself.

In fact, the theorem is considerably more general than this and was not originally developed in the context of economics. The more general version of Brouwer theorem states that the mapping f needs only to be from a closed, compact, convex set onto itself for f to have a fixed point.

Applying Brouwer fixed point theorem to the exchange economy example and using (1) will produce the following relation:

$$\exists p_i^* \ s.t. (1+\sum_i \max\left(0, g_i\left(p^*\right)\right) = p_i^* + \max\left(0, g_i\left(p^*\right)\right)$$

If c is defined as follows:

$$c = 1 + \sum_i \max(0, g_i\left(p^*\right))$$

The equation can be simplified as follows:

$$p_i^*\left(c-1\right) = \max\left(0, g_i\left(p^*\right)\right)$$

Therefore, the value of c must be $c \geq 1$, so there are two possibilities.

3.2.1   *First possibility suggests that* $c > 1 \Rightarrow max\left(0, g_i\left(p^*\right)\right) > 0 \forall i \rightarrow$

$$\sum_i p_i^* g_i\left(p^*\right) > 0 \, as \, p^* \geq 0$$

But this says that the value of excess demand is strictly greater than 0, which contradicts Walras' law.

3.2.2   Thus, second possibility assumes that $c = 1$

$$\Rightarrow p_i^* = p_i^* + max\left(0, g_i\left(p^*\right)\right)$$

So $max\left(0, g_i\left(p^*\right)\right) = 0$

$$\Rightarrow g_i\left(p^*\right) \leq 0 \forall i$$

In other words, there is an equilibrium.

What exactly have we shown? If we could find a fixed point to the mapping given by eq. 1, then we would have found an equilibrium price vector to our exchange economy. The question now is how to find this equilibrium. To proceed with this question, a completely new topic, vector labeling, needs to be discussed, which starts with integer labeling.

3.3   Integer labeling

In order to move towards the solution to the fixed-point problem, an introduction of a completely unfamiliar concept, integer labeling, is needed. No use of any calculus or, indeed, differentiability. Rather, the methodology will move in discrete steps towards a "best" approximation of an equilibrium, using a particular subdivision of the price simplex. Consider the diagram in the next section that shows a three-dimensional price simplex (Figure 3.5). That is, all points on the two-dimensional faces of the simplex have coordinates that sum to 1. The vertices of the simplex are given by 1 = (1, 0, 0), 2 = (0, 1, 0), 3 = (0, 0, 1). Any vector in the interior of the simplex is given by

$$\alpha = \left(\alpha_1, \alpha_2, \alpha_3\right) s.t. \sum \alpha_i = 1$$

The "correctly oriented" sub-simplex can be considered as a sub-triangle whose sides are parallel to the larger simplex. Thus, the triangle S_1 in the picture would be correctly oriented, while S_2 would not be. What would characterize an interior point of S_1? It would appear to be those points whose third coordinate is greater than α_3, whose second coordinate is greater than α_2, and whose first coordinate is greater than α_1.

More formally, how can one define such a "correctly oriented" sub-simplex? It would appear that the elements in it are characterized by the following:

No vector has 0 component.

No 2 vectors have the same i^{th} component.

Thus, for example, no vectors on the sides α_1, α_2 have the same third coordinate as the vectors on the side α_3. The following question will lead to a simple characterization of a correctly labeled sub-simplex.

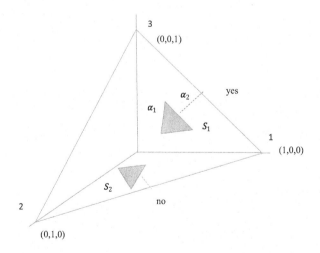

Figure 3.5 Three-dimensional price simplex with "correctly and incorrectly oriented" sub-simplices

Question: can you take n vectors and draw a simplex with each side passing through only one of the n vectors? So suppose there is an n-dimensional that is characterized by the vectors given in the matrix here.

$$\begin{bmatrix} x_1^1 & \cdots & x_1^n \\ \vdots & \vdots & \vdots \\ x_n^1 & \cdots & x_n^n \end{bmatrix}$$

The following lemma will characterize the correct labeled sub-simplex.

Lemma: the smallest element in each row must lie in different columns.

As a counterexample, look at the matrix in the next section. The smallest element in each row is given by the symbol – above the row element. Clearly the elements in each column sum to 1, but the smallest elements in the first and third row lie in the first column.

$$\overline{.4} \quad .5 \quad .7$$
$$.5 \quad .2 \quad \overline{.1}$$
$$\overline{.1} \quad .3 \quad .2$$

This does not work, so if the lemma is correct, then this matrix would not form a correctly labeled sub-simplex.

Proof of lemma:

Necessary as:

$$x_i^j \geq a_i \ \forall i$$

$$x_i^j = a_i \ for \ some \ i$$

$$x_i^k = a_i \ \forall \ other \ k$$

Sufficient: obvious (look at the correctly and incorrectly oriented sub-simplices in Figure 3.5).

The concept introduced in the next section is critical in the computational methodology: **a primitive set.**

3.4   Primitive sets

Definition: a primitive set

A primitive set is a sub-simplex, as in Figure 3.5, that

1. satisfies the lemma;
2. no other vectors lie in the interior of the set.

Intuitively, the primitive set is a correctly oriented sub-simplex that is so small that no other vectors lie inside it. Thus, the sub-simplex in the Figure 3.6 would not be a primitive set since there is an interior vector.

The next step is to define how to move from one primitive set to another. More specifically:

Question: what happens if there is a primitive set $x^1 \cdots x^n$ and one column is being removed and replaced by a new column? First, the definition of a primitive set should be extended, as summarized in the next section and depicted in Figure 3.7.

Extended definition of primitive set: a primitive set may include sides of the simplex.

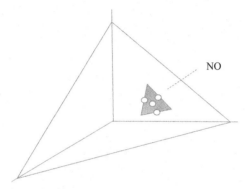

Figure 3.6 Incorrectly defined primitive set

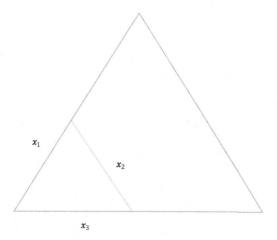

Figure 3.7 Primitive set according to extended definition

This extended definition allows to consider the primitive set in the next section and to replace the side represented by the vector x_3. Intuitively, the side is slid in parallel to itself to x_3. Hence x_3' has the second smallest third coordinate.

Replacement step

This setup brings forward a critical theorem.

Theorem: suppose $(x^1,\ldots,x^n)$ is a primitive set. If one vector is replaced, then there is always a new vector replacing it, giving a primitive set unless it has three sides on the boundary of the simplex.

The numerical example here demonstrates the discussed in more details. This would be a four-dimensional simplex (Table 3.1).

Thus, the first four vectors represent the sides of the simplex. Vector x4 is the interior vector with the largest first coordinate. There are therefore no other vectors in the interior of the properly oriented primitive set formed by x1, x2, x3, x4 (Table 3.2).

The smallest element in each row lies in a different column (shown by the underlining); therefore, Primitive Set 1 satisfies the lemma defined earlier.

The removal of x2 from the primitive set, which has a minimum element in the second row, will result in the following:

x3 has third coordinate constant.

x4 has fourth coordinate constant.

x5 has second coordinate constant since it now has the smallest element in that row.

How should x2 be replaced? A look at all remaining vectors determines that

x3 > 0, x4 > 0, x5 > 0.1 and the largest value for x1. Why is the largest value for x1 required? If the largest x1, then there will be a vector "inside" the

Table 3.1 Replacement of a vector

0	19	18	17	0.7	0.6	0.2	0.1	0.21	0.5	0.3
20	0	18	17	0.1	0.2	0.4	0.3	0.39	0.01	0.15
20	19	0	17	0.1	0.09	0.2	0.41	0.31	0.19	0.15
20	19	18	0	0.1	0.11	0.2	0.19	0.09	0.3	0.4
x1	x2	x3	x4	...						xN

Table 3.2 Primitive Set 1 (there are many others)

19	18	17	<u>0.7</u>
<u>0</u>	18	17	0.1
19	<u>0</u>	17	0.1
19	18	<u>0</u>	0.1
x2	x3	x4	x5

primitive set, which violates the definition of a primitive set. Then, vector x6 will emerge.

The question now is, if this replacement step is continued, where one vector is removed, then the row with a minimum element is replaced with another vector that has the largest element in the remaining row, will the process somehow come to an end? That is, if there is a possibility to arrive at a primitive set for which it is no longer possible to make a replacement step? To answer this question, which will be essential to the computation of equilibrium, we need to extend some concepts.

Note

1 Brouwer, L. E. J. 1952. An Intuitionist's Correction of the Fixed-Point Theorem on the Sphere. *Proceedings of the Royal Society, London*, A213, 1–2.

4 Fixed points, continued

This chapter explains the essential ideas behind the computational methodology that will be used. The particular methodology developed here, simplicial subdivisions with integer labeling, is no longer used as a computational technique. However, it forms the basis of current fixed point computational methods, such as Merrill's (1972) algorithm, and it has the advantage of being relatively easy to describe. Then, Brouwer theorem can be constructively proven after the development of a theorem about achieving a completely labeled primitive set. The final section shows how equilibrium in an exchange economy can be immediately derived, once the knowledge on how to solve for the fixed point in Brouwer's theorem is gained. The discussion here will not be developing mathematically rigorous proofs of these results, but those will be derived in intuitive ways.

4.1 Simplicial subdivisions

Consider Figure 4.1, that represents a three-dimensional simplex with a number of interior points (vectors). Since every such point on the surface of the simplex is a vector, whose coordinates sum to 1, they represent different relative prices. Then the following theorem can be deduced:

> *Theorem*: suppose that each vector in the list $(x^1 \ldots x^n, \ldots, x^{n+k})$ is labeled with one of the first n integers. The only restriction is that x^i, the ith side, has label i. Then there exists a primitive set, where each side of which has a different label. The resulting primitive set is referred to as "completely labeled."

Proof: the basic idea is to construct a specific sequence starting with $n-1$ sides. The sequence does not cycle and ends only when all labels are different.[1]

It starts with a corner, as in Figure 4.1. Then x^j must be the vector with the largest first coordinate. If its label = 1, then the set is complete.

Otherwise, the vector with the same label will be removed.

If $x^{j'}$ has label 1, then the set is complete. Otherwise, the process will continue doing this "replacement" step.

DOI: 10.4324/9780429295485-4

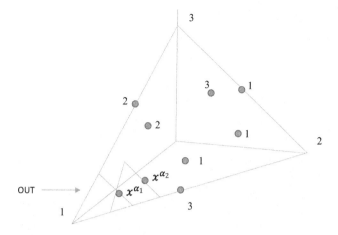

Figure 4.1 Three-dimensional simplex with a number of interior points

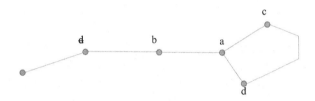

Figure 4.2 Choice of sides in a primitive set of simplex

At each step there are three possible situations:

1. None of the vectors have label 1.
2. All of the vectors have different label except one pair with the same label.
3. One of the identical labels has just come in.

The process of moving through the surface of the simplex replacing sides in this well-defined way will continue. It can only stop when each side of the selected primitive set has a different label. There are only a finite number of primitive sets on the simplex, since they have a discrete size. Hence after a finite number of steps, the process must end, assuming there is a proof that there is no cycling; that is, the steps never return to where they were before. Consider Figure 4.2.

What would this mean diagrammatically? At primitive set d, l_d will be removed, as there are two such labels. Then it will arrive back at primitive set a. But then,

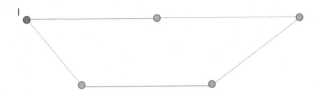

Figure 4.3 Conceptual inconsistency on having two ways out

now there are two elements with label l_a, and the diagram would seem to say that there were two ways out of a, either to c or to d. But by construction, there was only one way in and one way out of l_a, therefore there is no way out to l_d. Hence the only possibility for cycling would be Figure 4.3.

However, the option in Figure 4.3 is impossible since it would mean that there were two ways out of the initial corner. But this is impossible as one of the initial sides cannot be removed.

Thus, the discussed algorithm will arrive at a completely labeled primitive set without cycling. Another way of looking at this comes from an illustration due to Scarf (1973). Consider the story in the next section.

4.2   The house with two doors

Suppose we have a house with lots of rooms (Figure 4.4). There is one entrance to the house (point D). Every room has two doors. Then there must be a separate exit to the house.

Thus, no matter how the doors in the rooms are arranged, as long as there are two doors in each room, and there is only one door into the house, then there is not only a door into the house but also a well-defined path to leave the house. That is:

1. Enter the house by the front door (point D).
2. Exit the room you are now in by the only other door in the room.
3. You are now in a new room. This room has two doors. You came in through one door, so exit through the other.
4. Continue moving room to room in this manner. There are a finite number of rooms, so you must either eventually exit the house, or return to a room where you have already been.
5. But returning is not possible, by the previous argument, so the only option left is to exit after a finite number of steps.

This chapter has arrived to its key result, Brouwer fixed point theorem. Originally, the theorem was proved by a contradiction. Thus, if there was no fixed point to the mapping of the simplex onto itself, then the outcome would eventually arrive at a logical contradiction. This is not acceptable, so the conclusion is that there must be a fixed point.

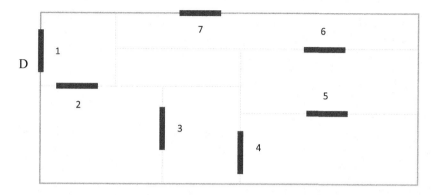

Figure 4.4 House with two doors

In current context, this result, while good to know, is not useful since it is needed to be able to find the fixed point, not just know that one exists. Therefore, the following construction of a sequence of steps will lead, after a finite number of steps, to the fixed point.

4.3   Brouwer's theorem: a constructive proof

Suppose that f is a mapping $f : S \rightarrow S$

$$y_1 = f_1(x_1,\ldots,x_n)$$

$$\vdots$$

$$y_n = f_n(x_1,\ldots,x_n)$$

Take a set of vectors $x^1,\ldots, x^k$ on the price simplex S.
  Give the vector x^j a label in the following way:
  For each vector x^j, calculate each dimension of $f(x^j) - x^j$. That is, compute the vector:

$$f_1(x^j) - x_1^j,\ldots, f_n(x^j) - x_n^j$$

We must have the following:

$$\Sigma f_i(x^j) = \Sigma x_i^j = 1$$

Since both $\{f_i\}$ and $\{x_i\}$ lie on the simplex.

$$\Rightarrow f_i(x^j) - x_i^j \geq 0 \text{ for some i.}$$

So give x^j the label i. If there is more than one value for i, then choose the one with the lowest index. Using the same two-door argument as before, this ends up with a primitive set with every face having a different label. That is:

$$f_i(x) - x_i \geq 0$$

for some x in the primitive set.

Now suppose that the primitive sets become very small. That is, the $\{x_i\}$ become a convergent limit so that $(x^j) \to x^*$ where x^* is a single point. Then there is

$$f_i(x^*) \geq x_i^* : \forall i$$

But

$$\sum f_i(x^*) = \sum x_i^* = 1$$

$$\Rightarrow f_i(x^*) = x_i^* : \forall i$$

This is the desired outcome, namely, that f has a fixed point, x_i^*.

If now the excess demand mapping discussed in the previous chapter is utilized and this simplex method is used, this will constructively derive the equilibrium prices for an exchange economy. However, there are a few issues that make the solution somewhat more complex than described here. First, passing to the limit x^* is not really as easy as described previously, as a constructive method have not been given for doing so. That is, it is not clear just what the limit properties of the integer labeling are when the fineness of the grid on the simplex approaches infinity. Nonetheless, this result on the convergence properties of the algorithm has been rigorously proven.

Yet another significant issue arises from the fact that the dimension of the problem (number of prices) causes the computational time to rise geometrically. Hence, in a model with a large number of commodities, the time to convergence could become prohibitively long, even on a very fast computer. The currently used method (Merrill's algorithm) allows to start anywhere in the price simplex. Hence, the prior information can be used, and there is no need to start from the corner of the price simplex. An additional feature of this algorithm is that it continuously shrinks the fineness of the grid on the price simplex as it converges to an equilibrium. Thus, the start is with the grid having relative prices "far" apart. When the algorithm achieves an equilibrium approximation on that grid, it then automatically shrinks the distance between relative prices on the new grid and finds a new best approximation. This shrinking grid methodology will be addressed in more details later. For now, a concluding note is that it provides extraordinary speed increases.

Note

1 The idea comes from Lemke and Howson (1964).

5 The linear economy and Kakutani's theorem

Let us recall Chapter 4 which considered only a pure exchange economy. Since the present objective is to develop a model for policy analysis, the discussion in that chapter constructs a strong basis, but it does not offer a useful final product. Real economies have both consumers and producers, and a market clearing equilibrium must incorporate the notion of price-variable supply. What are the intuitive problems in incorporating production? Perhaps the most basic such problem arises because the application almost invariably uses production functions which exhibit constant returns to scale (CRS). As it is known from basic micro theory, a CRS requires a production to realize zero profits in order to operate. If a particular set of relative prices results in a positive profit, then the production function will operate at infinity. If production function realizes a loss at those prices, then it does not operate. Finally, suppose the used algorithm calls off relative prices at which a production function makes zero profits. Then the level of production is indeterminate and that would also result in indeterminate excess demand. What to do?

5.1 The indeterminacy of output in an economy with linear production

How to extend the analysis to an economy with production? First, conduct an assessment to see whether it would be relatively easy to add production if production functions exhibit increasing returns to scale. Let us begin by returning to the example of a pure exchange economy. As before:

Define the production as a function of price, $f_i(p)$, where

$$f_i(p) = \frac{p_i + \max\left(0, g_i(p)\right)}{1 + \sum max\left(0, g_i(p)\right)}$$

If $f_i(p) \geq p_i \Rightarrow p_i$ *has label i*, then $f_i(p)$ can substituted for p_i, where

$$\frac{p_i + \max\left(0, g_i(p)\right)}{1 + \sum max\left(0, g_i(p)\right)} \geq p_i$$

DOI: 10.4324/9780429295485-5

Hence:

$$p_i + max\left[0, g_i(p)\right] \geq p_i\left[1 + \Sigma max\left(0, g_i(p)\right)\right]$$

This must be true for at least one value of i, as if it were not true then f would not lie on the simplex.

5.2 An application to an exchange economy

Suppose that the utility of the ith consumer $\left(U^i(x)\right)$ is given by a Cobb-Douglas function, which depending on elasticities $\left(\alpha_1, ..., \alpha_n\right)$ reflects a respective preference of the consumer for various goods $\left(x_1, ..., x_n\right)$:

$$U^i(x) = x_1^{\alpha_1} ... x_n^{\alpha_n}$$

His initial endowment, such as capital and labor, is given by the following:

$$r^i = \left(r_1^i, ..., r_n^i\right)$$

So his income is as follows:

$$I^i(p) = \sum_{j=1}^{N} p_j r_j^i$$

Hence, for any price and endowment, the demand for goods for consumer i is given by the following:

$$d^i(p) = \alpha_1 \frac{I^i(p)}{p_1}, ..., \alpha_N \frac{I^i(p)}{p_N}$$

Aggregate demand is derived through summing individual demand across all consumers and is determined as follows:

$$D(p) = \sum_{i=1}^{I} d^i(p)$$

Next, excess demands are calculated as the difference between the aggregate demand and aggregate endowment:

$$g(p) = D(p) - r$$
$$= \left(D_1(p) - r_1, ..., D_N(p) - r_N\right)$$

As before, a matrix of N price vectors is determined, where each of the columns has a different label. Hence, a matrix of N price vectors is shown here:

$$\begin{bmatrix} p_1^1 & \cdots & p_1^N \\ \vdots & \ddots & \vdots \\ p_N^1 & \cdots & p_N^N \end{bmatrix}$$

The next step is to add production functions.

Single valued production functions

Suppose, as a simple first case, the production functions exhibit strictly decreasing returns to scale. Let h^j denote the jth such function, where

$$h^j(p) = h_1^j(p), \dots, h_N^j(p)$$

and $h_i^j(p) > 0$ if good i is a net output, and $h_i^j(p) < 0$ if good i is a net input.

Then aggregate supply, which is a function of price, is well defined and is given by

$$S(p) = \sum_{j=1}^{N} h^j(p)$$

This allows to add the concept of aggregate output in the assessment of excess demand, which can be estimated as follows:

$$g(p) = D(p) - S(p) - r$$

The use of the same labeling method as before allows to approximate an equilibrium.

Summary so far

The method outlined previously provides necessary tools to solve for the equilibrium of an economy with any number of consumers with standard utility functions and any number of production functions, as long as they exhibit strictly decreasing returns to scale.

What is missing?

5.3 Why Brouwer theorem will not work, and what will?

Typically, production functions, as estimated with real-world data, exhibit constant returns to scale (CRS) and hence do not have single valued supply responses. For example, input-output matrices are linear, while Cobb-Douglas, constant elasticity of substitution (CES), and other production functions are CRS. There are a number of reasons for this. Mainly, estimation of a production function does not cover a range of outputs such that factor inputs become binding constraints. Thus, over the range of observations, the function appears to be CRS. Alternatively, over the range of observations, the practitioner may linearize so as to generate a CRS function.

Suppose now that the analysis is dealing with a CRS function, let $\pi(p)$ denote the per unit profit of this function at prices p. If

$\pi(p) < 0$, *then firm does not operate*

$\pi(p) > 0$, *then firm operates at* ∞

$\pi(p) = 0$, *then firm operates from 0 to* ∞

Accordingly, only the production function defined in the final case will produce a meaningful output. However, this case will not give a single valued function for excess demand, as described previously. This will cause problems in trying to use the integer labeling and Brouwer theorem as described previously. Therefore, there is a need to have a methodology to deal with the sort of set-valued outcome generated by the $\pi(p) = 0$ case in the previous section. These outlined observations will lead to Kakutani's fixed point theorem.

5.4 The concept of vector labeling and its application

This section will begin by making a rather brief statement of Kakutani's theorem.

Kakutani's theorem: a very brief overview

The concept of vector labeling is introduced in the following way.

Define a mapping, which takes $p^j \to a^j$

Where a^j is an $N \times 1$ vector that does not necessarily lie on the simplex. The only restriction is in the mapping of prices that are on the side of the simplex. Here:

$$p^1 \to (1,0\ldots0)$$

$$\vdots$$

$$p^N \to (0,0\ldots1)$$

This will end up with a matrix A where:

$$A = \begin{array}{ccc} p^1,\ldots,p^N & p^{N+1},\ldots, & p^{N+k} \\ 1,0,\ldots0 & a_1^{N+1},\ldots, & a_1^{N+k} \\ \vdots & \vdots & \vdots \\ 0,0,\ldots1 & a_N^{N+1},\ldots, & a_N^{N+k} \end{array}$$

Thus, a vector that lies in the interior of the price simplex is associated with, for now, a random vector a^j, and there are no restrictions upon a^j. The next step is to define a new vector b as follows:

$$b = (b_1,\ldots,b_N)$$

Again, there are essentially no constraints upon the coefficients of b.

Then use the following definition:

Definition: $\{j_1,\ldots,j_N\}$ form a *feasible basis* if

$Ay = b$ has a unique solution with $\{y^j\} \geq 0$

$y_j = 0$ *unless* $j \in \{j_1,\ldots,j_N\}$

Hence a feasible basis is defined as the solution to the linear programming problem

$$Ay = b$$

With the constraint that there are no values $y_j < 0$. This would not be the case with a random such linear programming problem.

As follows, to introduce two basic theorems:

Theorem 1: Let p^j be associated with the jth column of A. Assume also that the vectors y such that $Ay = b$ is bounded. Then there exists a primitive set whose associated columns form a feasible basis.

Thus, there is a primitive set on the price simplex that has associated with it a unique solution to the linear programming problem. In order to arrive at Theorem 1, a path to arrive at this primitive set needs to be constructed. The methodology will be the equivalent of the replacement step with integer labeling. However, here it will be developed with the use of vectors. We have the following theorem:

Theorem 2: Given a feasible basis $\{j_1,\ldots,j_N\}$ for $Ay = b$. Assume that b cannot be represented with fewer than N columns of A. Assume also that y s.t. $Ay = b$ is bounded. If we want to bring the column $j^* \notin (j_1,\ldots,j_N)$ into the basis, then there exists a unique column to be replaced.

As mentioned previously, this is the equivalent of the replacement step with integer labeling. As before, assume that a primitive set consists of $N-1$ price vectors on the sides of the simplex, and one interior price vector. Now the sides of the price simplex correspond to the unit vectors in the feasible basis. Hence, this correspondence is represented in the following way:

Primitive set : $2, 3,\ldots, N, j$
                    ↓ ↓   ↓
Feasible basis: $1, 2, 3,\ldots, N$

Suppose that $x^j \rightarrow a^j$

where symbol $\rightarrow$ represents correspondence.

Then a^j is introduced into the feasible basis. If column 1 is eliminated, then it is solved. Otherwise, the next step is as follows:

$2, 3, \ldots, *, \ldots, n, j, j'$
$1, 2, 3, \ldots, *, \ldots, n, j$

A complete correspondence will be achieved if j' = 1, and that will finalize the process.

This process will continue and can only finish if a^1 is eliminated or if p^1 comes into the primitive set. The proof that a complete correspondence will be achieved is again by the two-door argument to get no cycling. As before, there are only a finite number of primitive sets. Hence, we need to show that there is no recycling in solving the linear programming problem. This is done by a more complicated version of the two-door problem. We can now turn to Kakutani's theorem.

Kakutani's theorem

This discussion will start with the definition of the concept of upper-semicontinuity, which will be, for a set valued mapping, the equivalent of continuity for a single-valued function.

Suppose that

$$x \to \Phi(x)$$

is a set-valued mapping. The definition is as follows.

Definition

The mapping $x \to \Phi(x)$ is upper semicontinuous (USC) if:

$$x^1,\ldots,x^n \to x \, and \, \varphi^i \epsilon \, \Phi(x^i)$$

Assume that $\varphi^i \to \varphi$. Then $\phi \epsilon \, \Phi(x)$.

Example

As an economic example, assume that CRS is a production function $f(x)$ and for a given price vector p consider $\{x\}$ s.t. x yields 0 profits at p. That is:

$$y = f(x) \, s.t. \, \pi = p \cdot y = 0$$

Then since f is CRS, for any such x, then $\pi = \lambda p \cdot y = 0$ for any $\lambda > 0$.

Accordingly, if $x^1,\ldots,x^n \to x$ then $y^1,\ldots,y^n \to y$ and $p \cdot y = 0$.

Hence the profit-maximization mapping for a CRS function is upper semicontinuous.

We can now state Kakutani's theorem

Kakutani's theorem

Suppose that $x \to \Phi(x)$ is a mapping from $S \to S$ and is USC. Suppose also that for each x that $\Phi(x)$ is a non-empty, closed, convex set.

Then $\exists x^* \in \Phi\left(x^*\right)$

It should be clear that this is the set valued equivalent of Brouwer's theorem. We will not present a rigorous proof here. Rather, we will note that the constructive proof of Kakutani's theorem follows directly from Theorem 1. This will be very important for our application to economies with CRS in production, the solution to Kakutani will be the equilibrium for that economy.

It is worth noting that the original proof of Kakutani was a proof by contradiction, so it did not actually find the fixed point. Rather it showed that one must exist. This constructive proof actually finds the fixed point and hence the equilibrium.

6 Linear production technologies

Previous chapter illustrated how Kakutani's theorem can be used to compute an equilibrium of an economy with constant returns to scale production (CRS) functions. The focus of this chapter is on applications to the type of data which are available in real-world economics. More particularly, this section considers linear models of production. These are exemplified by input/output models of production, which are available for almost all major countries in the world. The demand side of the economy represents a system in which all consumers spend constant fractions of their income on each consumption good, although these fractions need not be uniform across consumers. Such data are typically available in social accounting matrices (SAM). These SAMs generally list multiple consumer categories, such as urban, rural, income quintiles, occupations, and so forth. For each category they list expenditures on each category of consumption as a share of the consumer's income. Such data enable the immediate use of a Cobb-Douglas utility function.

6.1 The importance of linear models of intermediate and final production

To proceed, three factors need to be further specified in the Walrasian model.

6.1.1 Production technology

This will usually be either neoclassical production functions or linear production functions (input-output is an example). There are a variety of reasons for the practical use of these structures. Most such reasons revolve around the notion that intermediate and final production structures are essentially assembly line processes. Thus, a production line for a bicycle has two tires, one seat, one handlebar, etc. There is no substitution between the inputs.

6.2 Substitution in factor inputs, linearity in intermediate and final production

6.2.1 On the other hand, there is possible substitution between factors of production. That is, the bicycle production process uses capital and labor to produce value

DOI: 10.4324/9780429295485-6

added. These factor inputs may be used in varying proportions, so for example, it could produce the bicycles using a few skilled craftsmen and lots of robots. Alternatively, it could produce the bicycles using simple tool and lots of workers. However, the intermediate and final recipe for bicycle remains unchanged: two tires, one seat, one handlebar, etc.

Another reason for such a specification of production is practical and similar to the justification for using I-O matrices: data availability. Essentially every country in the world has an I-O matrix of production, and these matrices are updated regularly to reflect the current technology of the country. Thus, for example, all 30 OECD countries have I-O matrices with uniform sectors, dimensions, and annual update years. Accordingly, if we are working on a CGE model of one, or a group of these countries, then much of our data work is already done.

6.2.2 The second key set of data that we need are consumption parameters. These are, for example, the utility weights in a Cobb-Douglas (CD) function. These weights would reflect the corresponding percentage of income spent on each commodity by a representative consumer. The data, depending on the functional form chosen for the underlying utility functions, might also include, for example, the elasticities of substitution in a constant elasticity of substitution (CES) utility function.

This type of consumption data is not uniformly available, but it is for a number of countries in the form of social accounting matrices (SAM). These are tables derived from household surveys, on a country-by-country basis. The social accounting matrices contain a number of items, but the most important from the researcher's point of view is a matrix that gives expenditure on each consumption good as a share of income for each consumer category. These shares can be taken directly to be the coefficients in Cobb-Douglas utility functions for each consumer type in the economy. This means that without any further data work, the researcher has constructed a system of demand for the economy. However, one additional set of data is necessary in order to determine levels of demand for each consumer. This is the initial distribution of assets described in the following section.

6.2.3 Initial distribution of assets. Empirically this means that only the distribution of income is not enough to proceed with the analysis, but also the sources of that income, including capital, labor, land, and other assets. In addition, when we think about the real world from which our data will come, we realize that significant wealth is inherited. Thus, the information on ownership of assets at the household level is another essential factor to consider. This can be difficult, since typical IO information is given only on the level of a single, aggregate household. Thus, all capital and labor wealth is attributed to a single agent. This approach would, however, preclude the consideration of distributional impacts of government policies. Accordingly, the analysis, which calls for the distributional and relative welfare impacts of policies, will be limited to countries that have fairly detailed SAMs.

6.3   The steps to a fixed point solution to an economy with linear production and (almost) arbitrary consumer preferences

Let us now turn to computational details. Suppose we have an $n \times n + k$ dimensional linear production technology B given by

$$
B = \begin{bmatrix} -1,0, & \cdots & 0,b_{1,n+1},\ldots,b_{1,n+k} \\ \vdots & \ddots & \vdots \\ 0,0, & \cdots & -1,b_{n,n+1},\ldots,b_{n,n+k} \end{bmatrix}
$$

What is the interpretation of this matrix? The number of rows, n, represents the number of goods in the economy. The number of columns represents the number of production activities. One may think of these as being individual factories. The first n columns, the negative identity matrix, may be thought of as disposal activities. By this we mean throwing away a quantity of the good. The remaining k columns are actual production processes, each of which is linear with fixed coefficients.

Then production is given by

$$B \cdot y \; s.t. \; y \geq 0$$

That is, y is a vector representing levels at which each activity of production operates.

Assume that prices are normalized s.t.

$$\sum_{i=1}^{n} p_i = 1$$

Here, the assumption is that only relative prices matter so that there is no money illusion, which allows to normalize prices.

What does this mean, in practical terms? Money illusion would mean that if the wage of households rises by 10 percent while all other prices of goods and services rise by 10 percent, then they believe to be richer. Not having money illusion would mean that the households understand that they are not richer, and they do not change their consumption pattern. In contrast, having money illusion would mean that households do think they are richer and therefore consume more. There are important policy implications if people do, indeed, suffer from money illusion. In this case, a monetary expansion that leads to equal inflation in both wages and commodity price would still yield an increase in consumption and hence in growth.

In addition to requiring no money illusion, the Walras' law hold. Intuitively, Walras' law says that there is a circular flow of income in that the value of demand equals the value of supply. This circular flow holds whether the economy is in equilibrium or not. More specifically, even though the following condition may not hold:

$$S_i = D_i$$

For some value of i, the following condition still must hold:

$$\sum P_i S_i = \sum P_i D_i$$

The intuition is simple. A consumer spends income, and the income they spend then goes to other consumers who spend it.

Demand functions can be any continuous (actually upper semicontinuous) convex functions. In fact, the work in this setting does not require utility functions, but it can use preference orderings. The work with data allows a direct handling of estimated demand functions.

An equilibrium is p^*, y^* s.t.

A) $D\left(p^*\right) = B \cdot y^* + r$ where r is the vector of initial allocations.

B) $\sum_i p_i^* b_{ij} \leq 0 : \Delta j$

C) $\sum_i p_i^* b_{ij} = 0 : if \ y_j > 0$

We then have a simple theorem:

Theorem: suppose that the set of y s.t.

$$B * y + r \geq 0 \ and \ y \geq 0$$

is bounded. Then there is a p^* that satisfies the conditions for an equilibrium.

The proposed is an existence theorem, but it does not explain actually how to compute the equilibrium. The next step is to come up with a methodology that will generate a path to the equilibrium. Recall that we are dealing with a linear production technology; hence this is a very specialized and relatively simple case. This can be solved in a series of steps.

1. For any price p^j, search through the technology matrix B and calculate profits for each activity (column). That is, calculate the following:

$$\pi_k^j = \sum_{i=1}^{n} p_i^j b_{i,k}$$

where π_k^j is the profit made by column k at price vector p_i^j. The subscript i refers to the row dimension of the price and the row coefficient of the column b. Then choose a particular column of the production matrix in the following way.

2. Let π_k^j be the maximum profit over all columns. Now construct a new matrix A s.t.

$$A = \begin{array}{cccc} p^1 & p^n & p^{n+1} & p^{n+k} \\ \begin{bmatrix} 1,0, & \cdots & 0, a_{1,n+1}, \ldots, a_{1,n+k} \\ \vdots & \ddots & \vdots \\ 0,0 & \cdots & 1, a_{n,n+1}, \ldots, a_{n,n+k} \end{bmatrix} \end{array}$$

In constructing this matrix, price vector p^j is associated with the column a_{ij}. For now, the columns a_{ij} are unknown. The next step will be to fill in these blanks. The first step is look at profitability.

Suppose $\pi_k^j > 0$ then set

$$(a_{1,j},\ldots,a_{n,j}) = -\left(b_{1,k},\ldots,b_{n,k}\right)$$

Suppose $\pi_k^j \leq 0$ then set

$$(a_{1,j},\ldots,a_{n,j}) = \left[d_1\left(p^j\right)\ldots d_n\left(p^j\right)\right]$$

This calculates the value of demand at price $\left(p^j\right)$.

The next step is to solve

$$A \cdot y = w$$

Where w is the vector of initial endowments.

At each step there is a correspondence:

$$\left\{p^{j_1},\ldots,p^{j_n}\right\} \leftrightarrow \left\{y_1,\ldots,y_n\right\}$$

That is,

$$\sum_{j=1}^{n} y_j a_{ij} = w_i$$

So that

$$\sum_{j=1}^{n} \alpha_j \cdot \begin{bmatrix} d_1\left(p^j\right) \\ \vdots \\ d_n\left(p^j\right) \end{bmatrix} = \begin{bmatrix} w_1 \\ \vdots \\ w_n \end{bmatrix} + \sum_{j=1}^{n} y_j \begin{bmatrix} b_{1,j} \\ \vdots \\ b_{n,j} \end{bmatrix}$$

Now let the price grid shrink to a single price p^*, which will result in the following:

$$\sum_{j=1}^{n} \alpha_j \cdot \begin{bmatrix} d_1\left(p^*\right) \\ \vdots \\ d_n\left(p^*\right) \end{bmatrix} = \begin{bmatrix} w_1 \\ \vdots \\ w_n \end{bmatrix} + \sum_{j=1}^{n} y_j \begin{bmatrix} b_{1,j} \\ \vdots \\ b_{n,j} \end{bmatrix}$$

It is then possible to show that

$$\sum_{j=1}^{n} \alpha_j = 1$$

This will result in the following:

$$\begin{bmatrix} d_1\left(p^*\right) \\ \vdots \\ d_n\left(p^*\right) \end{bmatrix} = \begin{bmatrix} w_1 \\ \vdots \\ w_n \end{bmatrix} + \sum_{j=1}^{n} y_j \begin{bmatrix} b_{1,j} \\ \vdots \\ b_{n,j} \end{bmatrix}$$

Thus, supply equals demand where activity levels are given by the vector $\left\{y_j\right\}$.

To summarize the previously defined method: we have found a price vector p^* such that utility maximizing consumers optimize at that price, subject to their own budget constraints. Their aggregate demands are then equal to the initial factor supplies, plus the net outputs of the productions technology. In addition, all the activities of the production technology that are in use at equilibrium have zero profits at the equilibrium prices.

We have thus constructed a competitive equilibrium, whereas we had previously only shown that one existed. This is, of course, the methodology we need to implement practical applications of the general equilibrium model.

7 Numerical solutions; some examples

This chapter provides three basic examples of solving general equilibrium models using numerical techniques. All of these can be solved in some form using pencil and paper. Some of these are taken from popular textbooks on microeconomics. Readers are encouraged to set pencil to paper and to work through the numerical solutions to each problem. This allows us to walk through the process of setting up and solving a simple CGE model. The first example is an exchange model.

7.1 The exchange model

The exchange model is a useful starting place as it is often the starting place for most general equilibrium classes in microeconomic theory. This example considers a simple two good case which can be solved by hand, and then we will use a computer to solve for the same result. This will help develop some intuition into how to go about creating a program to solve for these results.

First, let us set up the problem, then we will delve into the two solution techniques. In this model there are two agents trading two goods. Sometimes this is referred to as a two-by-two pure exchange model. Note that this setup can be expanded to several goods and agents. The choice of two is determined by the relative ease of solving the problem by hand.

Suppose each of the two agents has preferences between the goods, and that goods 1 and 2 are represented by x_1 and x_2 respectively. Preferences can be represented by a utility function $U^i\left(x_1^i, x_2^i\right)$, and each has an initial allocation of goods w_1^i, w_2^i. Here i denotes the agent with this allocation and utility function. In this model the value i for agents 1 and 2 are denoted in superscripts by letters a and b, respectively. This allows to remove confusion between two agents and two goods. The sum of coefficients α, and $1-\alpha$ is restricted to 1, which implies a substitution elasticity between goods x_1^i and x_2^i of unity. The utility maximization problem for each agent is as follows:

$$U^i\left(x_1^i, x_2^i\right) = \alpha^i \ln\left(x_1^i\right) + \left(1 - \alpha^i\right)\ln\left(x_2^i\right)$$

$$\max \alpha^i \ln\left(x_1^i\right) + \left(1 - \alpha^i\right)\ln\left(x_2^i\right)$$

s.t.

DOI: 10.4324/9780429295485-7

$$p_1 x_1^i + p_2 x_2^i \le p_1 w_1^i + p_2 w_2^i$$

After taking the first order conditions, we can get demands for each good and consumer as a function of prices and initial allocations. The utility function is a basic Cobb-Douglas form, so demands are simply constant shares of income. Using demands we can get the following offer curves (OC^i) for each consumer:

$$OC^i = \left\{ \frac{\alpha^i}{p_1} \left(p_1 w_1^i + p_2 w_2^i \right), \frac{1-\alpha^i}{p_2} \left(p_1 w_1^i + p_2 w_2^i \right) \right\}$$

Now we need to assume some parameters and initial allocations. For agent 1 we assume $\alpha^a = 0.3$, $w_1^a = 10$, $w_2^a = 2$, and for agent 2 we assume $\alpha^b = 0.7$, $w_1^b = 2$, $w_2^b = 6$. Setting $p_1 = 1$ as our numeraire price, we can find the following solution to this problem. The best first step is to find the second price by using the assumption that supply will equal demand in equilibrium. To do this we add together the demands for good 1 from both agents and set it equal to the sum of allocations of good 1. This looks like:

$$\alpha^a w_1^a + \frac{\alpha^a}{p_1} p_2 w_2^a + \alpha^b w_1^b + \frac{\alpha^b}{p_1} p_2 w_2^b = w_1^a + w_1^b$$

Putting in the parameters we defined:

$$(0.3)(10) + (0.3)(2)p_2 + (0.7)(2) + (0.7)(6)p_2 = 10 + 2$$

Doing a few calculations, we get the following expression:

$$4.4 + 4.8 p_2 = 12$$

Solving for p_2:

$$p_2 = \frac{12 - 4.4}{4.8} \approx 1.58$$

Plugging this price in to the different demand functions and doing some calculations gives the following demands:

$$(x_1^a, x_2^a) = (3.95, 5.83); (x_1^b, x_2^b) = (8.04, 2.18)$$

Here, the price is determined first and then the allocations are derived by using the offer curves. The application of different allocations and parameters will allow to explore their effect on equilibrium. For example, an increase in the initial supply of good 2 may result in the price of that good to fall according to classical economic theory.

7.2 Three good CGE exchange model

This section covers another simple exchange model which focuses on the case with three goods and three consumers. As these models get larger with more parameters, it can become difficult to solve for closed-form solutions. Application of numerical techniques is useful at that point to be able to find solutions to difficult general equilibrium problems.

This example considers a three good exchange economy with three agents. Each agent has a Cobb-Douglas utility function with two parameters. The maximization problem is stated as follows:

$$\max \alpha^i \ln\left(x_1^i\right) + \beta^i \ln\left(x_2^i\right) + \gamma^i \ln\left(x_3^i\right)$$

subject to

$$p_1 x_1^i + p_2 x_2^i + p_3 x_3^i \le p_1 w_1^i + p_2 w_2^i + p_3 w_3^i$$

$$and \, \alpha^i + \beta^i + \gamma^i = 1$$

This is true for all three agents $i \in \{a, b, c\}$. Now we solve the agent's maximization problem and find the individual demand function for each agent. It is important to remember the objective of analysis at each step of the algorithm. The technique for solving these problems revolves around finding excess demands. For this problem initial allocations of each good will be assigned before the algorithm starts. While the algorithm is running, a vector of prices is generated at the start of each iteration. We then use those prices to find total quantity demanded for each good and then subtract the total allocations to form our vector of excess demands. Those excess demands are then fed back to the algorithm to generate a new vector of prices. So the task now is to find excess demands for a given initial allocation and price vector. Since the utility function is Cobb-Douglas, we can find the demand functions in the same way as before:

$$x_1^i = \frac{\alpha^i}{p_1}\left(p_1 w_1^i + p_2 w_2^i + p_3 w_3^i\right)$$

$$x_2^i = \frac{\beta^i}{p_1}\left(p_1 w_1^i + p_2 w_2^i + p_3 w_3^i\right)$$

$$x_3^i = \frac{\gamma^i}{p_1}\left(p_1 w_1^i + p_2 w_2^i + p_3 w_3^i\right)$$

Using these, we can now find the demands for every consumer for a given price vector. Since supplies of these goods are just the initial allocations, excess demands can be quite easily determined.

$$ex_j = \sum_{i \in \{a,b,c\}} (x_j^i - w_j^i) \quad , \quad j \in \{1, 2, 3\}$$

Where ex_j is the excess demand for good j. Since prices and initial allocations at every step of the algorithm are known, excess demands can be calculated for all goods at every step of the algorithm. Putting this all together we now turn to the code to write this program.

7.3 Writing the code

This section uses the example code "exchange.f90" in the Fortran subfolder named Exchange. The first 60 lines declare the variables to be used and then reads in and assigns the values from the file input.txt. All the code for this chapter and others may be downloaded from the publisher's website. The data used for this example is completely made up, and it can be changed in the input text file. Lines 61–76 set up the algorithm variables. Line 78 is where the main loop that finds the solution begins.

Since we have read in the allocations from the input file, we now need to assign the prices from the algorithm. We assign the price of the first good as the numeraire in our model. The rest of the prices are assigned in order from the primitive simplex.

```
numer = ps(2,jout) ! set numeraire
price(1) = ps(2,jout)/numer
price(2) = ps(3,jout)/numer
price(3) = ps(4,jout)/numer
```

Now we have prices for each good and initial allocations so we can calculate individual demands. Looping over all the agents in the model, we calculate their income first and then their demand for each good based on that income.

```
! Calculate income
income(i) = 0.
do j = 1,N
  income(i) = income(i) + price(j) * w(i,j)
end do
```

So each consumer gets an income that is based on their initial allocations and the prices called off at the beginning of each iteration in the algorithm. Using these incomes, we can now calculate their individual demands as follows:

```
! Calculate demands
do j = 1, N
  call cdDemand (d(i,j), price(j), alphas(i,j),
  income(i))
end do
```

Here we use a subroutine *cdDemand*, which just takes in prices, alphas, and income and returns a demand. The code for this subroutine can be found at the end of the program, but the code only calculates a constant share of income. Now we have the quantity demanded for every good for each consumer at the prices that have been called off. The last step is to calculate excess demands and see if they are close to zero. This is done in the following lines 112–117:

```
! Calculate excess demands
exOut = 0.
do j = 1, N
  ! This is just demand - supply
  exDem(j) = sum(d(:,j)) - sum(w(:,j))
  exOut = exOut + (exDem(j))**2
end do
```

In this *exDem* is a vector of excess demands. This is what we have been working toward. The second variable, *exOut* is a scalar that tells us how far from zero we are. If this number is smaller than our tolerance level, then we have found the equilibrium allocation, and we can terminate the loop. This condition is checked in lines 120–125. If this condition fails (we have not met the tolerance level), then we return to beginning of a new iteration where the excess demands from the previous iteration are used to find a new price vector. This loop is then continued until we converge to a sum of squared excess demands that is smaller than our tolerance level.

Now we can create the input file and run the program. For this exposition I assume agent *a* is the "rich" consumer with 15 units of each good, agent *b* is the "middle class" consumer with 5 units of each good, and agent *c* is the "poor" consumer with only 1 unit of each good. Utility parameters are also varied across the individuals. So the model is parameterized (Table 7.1).

Table 7.1 Parameters of the model

Initial Allocation:

Agent/Good	w_1	w_2	w_3
a	15	15	15
b	5	5	5
c	1	1	1

Parameters:

Agent/Parameter	α	β	γ
a	0.5	0.25	0.25
b	0.25	0.5	0.25
c	0.25	0.25	0.5

We can write this directly into the input file as follows:

```
15 15 15
5 5 5
1 1 1
0.5 0.25 0.25
0.25 0.5 0.25
0.25 0.25 0.5
```

Running this parameterization gives the equilibrium solution (Table 7.2):

Take, for example, agent *a* who had an initial allocation of 15 units of each good. He also, however, had a preference for more of good 1 than the other two agents. Adam Smith might say good 1 was *dearer* to him. As a result, we can see that he sells some of his allocation of goods 2 and 3 and uses that to buy more of good 1. Additionally, notice that he does not sell as much of good 3 as he does of good 2. This is because the price of good 3 is lower than the price of good 2. Thus good 2 is more expensive, and he buys less (sells more) of that good. Why is the price of good 2 smaller? This is because the middle-class consumer holds good 2 more dear, while the poor agent holds good 3 to be dearer. The middle-class agent has more buying power and can thus influence the price of good 2 more than the poor consumer can influence the price of good 3. General equilibrium effects like this might be ultimately ignored in partial equilibrium analyses.

7.4 Model of production with decreasing returns to scale

This section starts with an example of how to calculate the general equilibrium of a production economy. In this economy, a consumer with Cobb-Douglas utility supplies labor to a firm which operates a technology with decreasing returns to

Table 7.2 Equilibrium solution

Agent/Good	x_1	x_2	x_3
a	17.5	12.1	14.3
b	2.9	8.1	4.8
c	0.6	0.8	1.9
Total	21	21	21

Good:	x_1	x_2	x_3
Prices:	1.0	0.72	0.61

scale (DRS). This particular example is taken from Varian (1974), and the analytical solution, as well as other expositions, are included in that book. The discussion following provides a quick analytical solution. Readers can turn to Varian (1974) if their objective is a more in-depth review of how to solve for this problem.

Suppose the producer has a production function such that output is the square root of the input of labor. The firm's maximization problem is then given by the following:

$$\max \pi = \sqrt{L} - wL$$

Where L is the labor used by the firm and w is the wage rate paid to the worker. We normalize the price paid for output as 1.

The consumer then has a utility function over goods produced by the firm and the amount of leisure the worker takes. In this case, the utility function is Cobb-Douglas over leisure and goods with the parameter a. The worker has a set number of hours that she can devote to working or leisure. The number of hours the worker can allocate to either work or leisure is normalized to 1. Additionally, the consumer owns the firm, so she also receives all the profits in her income. The utility maximization problem for the consumer is as follows:

$$\max U(x, R) = a \ln x + (1 - a) \ln R$$

s.t.

$$x + wR = w + \pi$$

Where x is the amount of output good from the firm that the agent consumes, and R is the amount of leisure she "buys back" from the firm. Using the first order conditions and the constraints on feasible allocations, we get the following general equilibrium solution to the problem. The easiest starting point is to get the equilibrium wage and then work out the rest of the results from there. The equilibrium wage as a function of the parameter a is as follows:

$$w^* = \sqrt{\frac{2-a}{4a}}$$

$$\pi^* = \frac{1}{4w^*}$$

$$R^* = \frac{(1-a)}{w^*}\left(w^* + \pi^*\right)$$

$$x^* = a\left(w^* + \pi^*\right)$$

$$L^* = 1 - R^*$$

Using this system of equations describing our equilibrium we can find the equilibrium amounts given a parameter of the utility function. First, we need some economic meaning for the parameter *a*, and to do this, we can use a concept from basic consumer theory – the marginal rate of substitution. In this case, the marginal rate of substitution (MRS) between goods and leisure is as follows:

$$MRS_{xR} = \frac{\dfrac{\partial U}{\partial x}}{\dfrac{\partial U}{\partial R}} = \frac{\dfrac{a}{x}}{\dfrac{1-a}{R}} = \left(\frac{a}{1-a}\right)\left(\frac{R}{x}\right)$$

This suggests that the MRS is increasing with *a*. As *a* continues to increase, the amount of leisure the consumer is willing to give up for an extra unit of output also rises. This relationship is seen in the demand equations we derived as part of our characterization of equilibrium in this economy. Quantity demanded for leisure is decreasing with respect to *a* and quantity demanded for goods is increasing, for a fixed income amount.

Using the equations derived previously and the explanation of the utility function parameter, we can find relationships between variables and parameters in equilibrium. This essentially involves finding each variable as a function of parameters and seeing how the equilibrium evolves in response to different parameters. We will do this later when we compare our results to what we find computationally. For now, let us turn to the same problem, but now we will find the equilibrium with a computer instead of a pencil and paper.

7.5   Finding equilibrium computationally

Now that we have our basic analytical results, we want to be able to find the same equilibrium with a computer. For a problem like this, using a CGE approach is a bit like using a crane to crush a fly. In some cases, it is not necessary to write an entire CGE model just to solve one problem, but this will help for exposition. Finding general equilibrium for a simple problem in both manners will help you move from pencil and paper to keyboard and mouse. Using a CGE model to solve for general equilibrium is very *similar* to the analytical method. However, there are some differences in practice.

To solve a CGE model, remember that we are ultimately looking for *excess demands* for all scarce resources. In this model, the two scarce resources are labor and goods produced using that labor. First, the auctioneer calls of prices – wage and output price in this model. In the code, this comes from our algorithm. Lines 46 through 48 in the code define the prices for our system. In each iteration of the solution loop, a primitive simplex will be calculated. Excess demands for the current column being labeled (jout) must be calculated. We assign the vertex in the second row of each column to be the output price and the third row to be the wage. Note that we pick output prices as the numeraire as in the analytical model.

```
numer = ps(2,jout)
price = ps(2,jout)/numer
wage = ps(3,jout)/numer
```

After the prices have been called off, we need to solve for demands by the firm and profits that will be paid to the consumer. Using the first order conditions, we can write the following code to calculate demands for production:

```
laborDemand = 0.25*(price/wage)**2
outputSupply = sqrt(laborDemand)
profit = price*outputSupply - wage*laborDemand
```

At this point in the code, we have the demand for labor and the supply for output as well as the profits being sold to consumers. Using the profit, we can calculate the consumer's demand for output and leisure. Using the first order conditions, the code looks like the following:

```
laborSupply = 1 - (1-a)/wage * (wage + profit)
outputDemand = (a/price)*(wage+profit)
```

Now we have everything we need to solve for excess demands. We need to put them in a single variable so that the algorithm can calculate the new vertex. So the code to assign the excess demands is as follows:

```
exDem(1) = outputDemand - outputSupply
exDem(2) = laborDemand - laborSupply
```

Now excess demands have been calculated. If you are trying to write this code from scratch, try and run the program up to this point and see if you can get the correct answer. Using commands from Fortran and Julia to print variable values out on the screen is a very useful debugging technique. See, for example, Bezanson et al. (2017) for an introduction to the use of Julia in our context. Another commonly used language (package) for general equilibrium computation is described in Brooke et al. (1992). Once you have the excess demands calculating correctly, you can put all the code into a loop that terminates when a designated tolerance for excess demands has been reached. In the present code, we set this to 0.001. Using a smaller number will require more iterations but result in a more accurate result.

To compare our result to the analytical solution, we can look at the equilibrium response of variables to different parameter values. One good way to compare the models is using a graphing calculator (we use Excel to make the following graphs). Using the equation for wages from our pencil and paper solution:

$$w^* = \sqrt{\frac{2-a}{4a}}$$

We can graph the equilibrium relationship between w and a (Figure 7.1). Where a is on the horizontal axis and w is on the vertical. Using our CGE model we can run the equilibrium solution for multiple values of a. In the program, we calculate the equilibrium for values of a from 0.1 to 0.9. Taking the output from the table printed out at the end of the program, we can overlay the data on the existing graph (Figure 7.2).

Here the blue dots are the numerical approximation of this relationship from the solution we found on the computer. Clearly our result closely matches the analytical result as expected. This relationship could be approximated with a simple interpolation algorithm or any curve fitting algorithm.

This method is very much the building blocks for later models that incorporate more features. It starts with using calculus to optimize and find the demand functions for consumers and firms. We then use the algorithm to call off a set of prices and work through the functions to find quantities demanded and supplied for those prices that were called off. A new price vector is called off, and the program continues until a vector of prices is found that results in excess demands that are close to zero.

The figure is a graph that has a parameter on the horizontal axis and the wage variable on the vertical axis. A line decreases from the top left of the graph to the bottom right passing through the points (0.2, 1.5) and (0.4, 1). Nine larger points are overlayed on top of the line over the domain of the graph.

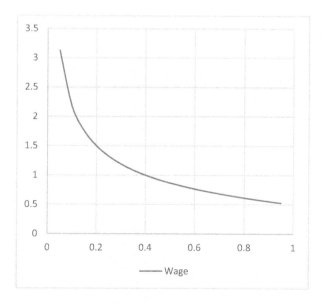

Figure 7.1 Equilibrium relationship between a and w

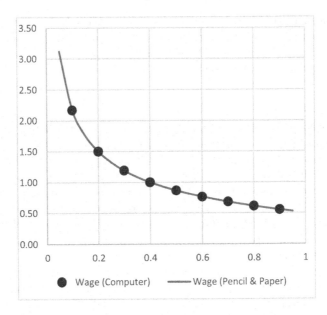

Figure 7.2 Comparison of analytical results and numerical approximation of the relationship

8 Production and government

In the previous chapter, we went through some simple examples of small economies that we can solve with CGE algorithms. We could also solve some of these by hand, so these were designed to help you understand the first steps in applying a general equilibrium model. In this section, we will discuss two important parts of the process of building a CGE model: production and government. Production is when firms create goods to sell to consumers, and a government imposes taxes on economic activity that redistributes the revenues to the consumer. The government may also spend money on behalf of the consumer.

To start, we will build another simple model that has only two sectors of the economy: a service-producing sector and a goods-producing sector. Each sector uses capital and labor as inputs and sells output to the consumer. We will include several types of taxes to explore the different ways one can introduce taxes to an economic model. First, we need to specify a production function for each firm. Again, to keep the model as simple as possible, we will be assuming some convenient functional forms. For production, we use the following Cobb-Douglas production function:

$$X_i \left(K_i, L_i \right) = \gamma_i K_i^{\alpha} L_i^{1-\alpha}$$

We use cost minimization to find the optimal demands for capital and labor. Since the exponents in the Cobb-Douglas function sum to unity, the production function exhibits constant returns to scale (CRS). This means that we can set up the following problem:

$$\min P_K k_i + P_L l_i$$

subject to

$$1 = \gamma_i k_i^{\alpha} l_i^{\beta}$$

In this case, the variables k_i and l_i are the capital and labor demands per unit of output. The problem specifically says, "What is the minimized cost of producing one unit of output?" The subscript i represents the two sectors in our economy such that

DOI: 10.4324/9780429295485-8

$i \in \{Services, Goods\}$. The only parameters we need to calibrate for this part are α and γ. Using first-order conditions, we can solve for input demands:

$$k_i^* = \left(\frac{1}{\gamma_i}\right)\left(\frac{\beta P_L}{\alpha P_K}\right)^\alpha$$

$$l_i^* = \left(\frac{1}{\gamma_i}\right)\left(\frac{\alpha P_K}{\beta P_L}\right)^\beta$$

For consumers, the problem is like previous models. Consumers maximize a utility function subject to an income constraint. Consumers buy firm output, X_1 and X_2, using income earned from selling capital and labor to the firms. In addition to choosing how many services and goods to consume, the representative consumer also decides how much labor to supply to firms in the market.

$$\max U\left(X_1, X_2, \overline{L}\right) = X_1^\theta X_2^{1-\theta} - v\frac{L^{1+\eta}}{1+\eta}$$

subject to

$$P_1 X_1 + P_2 X_2 = P_K W_K + P_L L$$

The functional form chosen is a linear combination of Cobb-Douglas utility from purchasing firm outputs and disutility from supplying labor to firms. The parameters we need to set for this section are θ, v, and η. The parameter θ is simply expenditure shares that we can get from a SAM. This functional form is useful since the parameter η turns out to be the Frisch elasticity of labor supply, which is commonly estimated in labor supply literature. Using first-order conditions, we can solve for consumer demands and labor supply:

$$L^* = \left(-\lambda\frac{P_L}{v}\right)^\eta, \ \lambda = \left(\frac{\theta}{P_1}\right)^\theta\left(\frac{1-\theta}{P_2}\right)^{1-\theta}$$

$$X_1^* = \frac{\theta}{P_1}\left(P_K W_K + P_L L^*\right)$$

$$X_2^* = \frac{1-\theta}{P_2}\left(P_K W_K + P_L L^*\right)$$

To solve this model, we use a method of dimension reduction to make it easier to solve. In models in previous chapters, all prices in the economy were called off, and excess demands were then calculated. In this case, one can instead use zero-profit conditions to calculate output prices from input prices. Zero-profit conditions indicate that marginal revenue must equal marginal cost in equilibrium, so equilibrium prices are just the sum of factor prices multiplied by per-unit optimal demands:

$$P_i = P_K k_i^* + P_L l_i^*$$

Taking factor prices called off by the algorithm and output prices calculated from marginal cost, we can solve the consumer's problem and solve for optimal demand for firm outputs. This allows us to reduce the size of the price vector we are solving on and, by extension, reduces the solution times for our program.

8.1 Calibrating our program

We will now go through the code in the folder "CRS," which contains two code files – "mainCRS.jl" and "mainCRS_tax.jl" – that contain the code for a constant returns to scale model without and with taxes, respectively. We will first start with the model without taxes to understand how we can use our model to numerically find an equilibrium.

Now that we have solved for the equations used to calculate excess demands, we can set the parameters. As mentioned previously, there are two sectors in this model: goods and services. We will calibrate our model to roughly represent the United States in 2019. We will use data from the Bureau of Economic Analysis, specifically their "Use" tables, and pull our labor supply elasticity from some econometric studies. First, the production parameters α and β are set to shares of labor and capital expenditures in the baseline data. According to the BEA, service-producing sectors paid about 65 percent of expenditures to labor, and goods-producing sectors paid about 50 percent of expenditures to labor. Thus, we get the first observation that service-producing sectors are more labor-intensive production processes. We are assuming that all firms are constant returns to scale, so α and β must sum to unity and so β is simply set as $1 - \beta$.

```
# alpha is labor; beta is capital
alpha[1] = 0.65 # Labor share in services
alpha[2] = 0.50 # Labor share in goods
beta[1] = 1 - alpha[1]
beta[2] = 1 - alpha[2]
```

To get the scale parameter γ, we assume that each dollar of output uses their respective shares of baseline capital and labor and solve for it.

```
# To calibrate the shift parameter in each equation,
# assume $1 of output can be obtained from the
respective
# shares of inputs in the data
gamma[1] = 1 / ((beta[1] ^ beta[1]) * (alpha[1] ^
alpha[1]))
gamma[2] = 1 / ((beta[2] ^ beta[2]) * (alpha[2] ^
alpha[2]))
```

Now we need to calibrate the consumer's utility function. For consumption, θ is simply the share of expenditure allocated to services in the baseline economy. Again, using the BEA tables, we find that about 65 percent of GDP is allocated to expenditure on services. Note that this takes into account all final output spending, which includes personal consumption, government outlays, and investment. First, calibrate the model to a specified benchmark GDP. This number is essentially arbitrary since we can scale up or down the rest of the numbers, but to get reasonable outputs we will use 20,000. This is about the GDP of the US in 2019 in billions of US dollars. Next, we will calibrate the baseline allocations of labor and capital based on their respective shares of income. According to BEA data, labor received about 60 percent of total income and capital received about 40 percent of total income, so set initial allocations of labor and capital to 60 percent of GDP and 40 percent of GDP respectively.

```
# Calibrate GDP
myGDP = 20000
# Calibrate labor and capital supplies
laborSupply = 0.6 * myGDP
capitalSupply = 0.4 * myGDP
```

To calibrate the labor supply curve, we first need a Frisch elasticity of labor supply. Estimates of this number vary widely, but for this model we will use 0.5. To match our model to baseline estimates of labor supply, we substitute the baseline level of labor into the labor supply function and solve for v.

```
# Now we can calibrate the labor supply function
eta = 0.5 # Elasticity of labor supply
nu = 1 / -(laborSupply ^ (1/eta))
theta = 0.65 # Share of consumer expenditure on
services
```

The rest of the code in this script is setting up vectors and parameters for the algorithm to solve the model. With our calibration complete, we move on to calculating excess demands.

8.2 Calculating excess demands

Given factor prices and the demand equations we found, we can find equilibrium excess demands for this economy. First, we use the algorithm to call off factor prices. In this model we select the price of capital as the numeraire. In the code, we use *wage* as the variable for the price of labor and *rent* for the price of capital. Again, we are using Merrill's algorithm to calculate equilibrium, so factor prices come from the primitive simplex:

```
global numer = ps[3,jout]
global wage = ps[2,jout]/numer # Price of labor
global rent = ps[3,jout]/numer # Price of capital
```

After setting the factor prices, we can solve for the optimal demands for factors using the equations for capital demands.

```
# Given prices calculate firm labor demands and firm
production
# Note that these demands are per unit of output
capitalDemand[1] = (1/gamma[1])*((wage*beta[1])/
(rent*alpha[1])) ^ alpha[1]
capitalDemand[2] = (1/gamma[2])*((wage*beta[2])/
(rent*alpha[2])) ^ alpha[2]
laborDemand[1] = (1/gamma[1])*((rent*alpha[1])/
(wage*beta[1])) ^ beta[1]
laborDemand[2] = (1/gamma[2])*((rent*alpha[2])/
(wage*beta[2])) ^ beta[2]
```

Here, the variables capitalDemand and laborDemand are two-element vectors representing the per-unit demands of capital and labor respectively. Each element within the vectors represents the firms for our two sectors: services and goods, so capitalDemand[1] is per-unit capital demand for the services sector. After calculating quantities demanded by consumers, we can find total demands for capital and labor.

To calculate consumer demands, we first need to determine the labor supplied to the market at the prevailing labor price, which allows us to calculate income for the consumer.

```
# Calculate labor supply
global laborSupply = (wage/-nu) ^ eta
# Calculate consumer demands
x[1] = (theta/price[1])*(rent*capitalSupply +
wage*laborSupply)
x[2] = ((1-theta)/price[2])*(rent*capitalSupply +
wage*laborSupply)
```

```
# Find total labor demands
totLaborDemand[1] = x[1] * laborDemand[1]
totLaborDemand[2] = x[2] * laborDemand[2]
totCapitalDemand[1] = x[1] * capitalDemand[1]
totCapitalDemand[2] = x[2] * capitalDemand[2]
```

Per-unit factor demands were found previously when calculating output prices, so total factor demands can be found by multiplying those numbers by output demands from the consumer.

Now, using the supplies of labor and capital, we can calculate excess demands and pass them back to the algorithm to generate a new price vector.

```
# Calculate excess demands
exDem[2] = sum(totCapitalDemand) - capitalSupply
exDem[1] = sum(totLaborDemand) - laborSupply
```

8.3   Running the model

After running the script, we print out the prices of factors and outputs, and we see that all prices are very close to unity. This is what we expected, as in the baseline we set all prices to unity. We can do some simple counterfactuals to see how our model responds to exogenous parameter changes. For example, suppose the labor in this economy falls by 20 percent. After running the model under this specification leads to output prices staying about the same, but the price of services increases slightly, and the price of goods falls slightly. The reason is immediately clear from the change in factor prices. The price of labor increases because it is relatively less abundant. For the service-producing firm, this is a relatively larger cost increase because they hire more labor in production. That cost gets passed through to the consumer in the form of a price increase on services. We can also do the opposite: suppose capital falls by 20 percent, what happens to the prices of capital, labor, services, and goods?

Another possible experiment is lowering the productivity of services. We can lower the γ parameter for services by 20 percent, and we see that the prices paid to factors falls for both labor and capital. The prices of output also change. The output price for services increases because the firm is not able to supply as many services to consumers. The output price of goods falls for two reasons: one is that goods are relatively more abundant, and the other is that income falls because factor prices fall and demands shift inward.

8.4   Adding taxes and transfers

Now that we have a simple model, we can now add taxes and government transfers to this model. The code that incorporates the following taxes is named "mainCRS_tax.jl," and it is in the CRS folder in the Julia folder. We will start with three types of taxes: personal income taxes, corporate income taxes, and consumption taxes. There are many different types of other taxes that CGE models can be used to analyze, but these are the most common in OECD countries. Income taxes are levied on supplies of capital and labor, and consumption taxes are levied on output prices. Taxes are collected by the government, which typically does two things with this revenue: transfers it back to consumers or spends it to produce goods like national defense or administration. We will deal with expenditures in another chapter, and in this model, we will focus on what happens when the government simply transfers these revenues back to the consumer in a lump sum fashion.

The introduction of taxes is not as simple as adding a wedge to the price vector, however, precisely because we are solving this in general equilibrium. Since governments transfer this money back to the consumer, the consumer needs to know total tax revenue to know their income. They need to know their income to decide about how much of each output to purchase. However, to know total tax revenue, the consumer needs to know how much output is purchased, and we have a simultaneity problem. As we show in the theory section, this problem was solved by Shoven and Whalley (1972) by adding another vertex to the price vector representing government revenues. We will take the same approach here.

Denote consumption taxes on services and goods as t_1 and t_2 respectively and denote income taxes on capital and labor as t_K and t_L. Additionally, we will denote the amount the consumer receives in government transfers as TR. This variable acts like a price and is called off by the algorithm we are using to solve the problem. The consumer's first-order conditions now become:

$$L^* = \left(-\lambda \frac{(1-t_L)P_L}{v}\right)^\eta, \lambda = \left(\frac{\theta}{P_1}\right)^\theta \left(\frac{1}{P_2}\right)^{1-\theta}$$

$$X_1^* = \frac{\theta}{P_1(1+t_1)}\left(P_K(1-t_K)W_K + P_L(1-t_L)L^* + TR\right)$$

$$X_2^* = \frac{1-\theta}{P_2(1+t_2)}\left(P_K(1-t_K)W_K + P_L(1-t_L)L^* + TR\right)$$

Next, we need to add in the corporate income tax. The corporate income tax is similar to the capital tax on income, in that it is a tax on payments to capital. In this case, however, we levy the tax on the firm paying the proceeds to capital rather than the household receiving income from capital. So the firm's equations become:

$$k_i^* = \left(\frac{1}{\gamma_i}\right)\left(\frac{\beta P_L}{\alpha P_K(1+t_i^c)}\right)^\alpha$$

$$l_i^* = \left(\frac{1}{\gamma_i}\right)\left(\frac{\alpha P_K(1+t_i^c)}{\beta P_L}\right)^\beta$$

In these equations, we denote the capital income tax with the superscript c, and we also differentiate tax rates by the subscript i. Thus, the tax rate can differ by industry.

Now that we have all the tax rates added into our equilibrium equations, we can do some final accounting again. The primary thing we need to add here is revenues collected from government. In this model we are assuming that the government runs a balanced budget. However, it is important to point out that this is more a mathematical imposition rather than a financial one. The government will always run a "balanced" budget in the sense that government outlays are equal to government revenues. The government can run deficits, which would require some government revenues to come from selling treasury notes. We cover this when discussing dynamic components of CGE models. The code to find the sum of revenues for the current example is as follows:

```
global R =
sum(cIncTax. * rent. * totCapitalDemand') +
# Corporate inc. tax rev.
capitalTax * rent * capitalSupply + # Capital
income revenue
wage * laborTax * laborSupply + # Labor income
revenue
sum(salesTax'. * price. * x) # Sales tax revenue
```

After calculating revenues, we take the difference between government outlays *TR* and revenues *R* and append them to the excess demands vector.

```
exDem[1] = sum(totLaborDemand) - laborSupply
exDem[2] = sum(totCapitalDemand) - capitalSupply
exDem[3] = R - TR
```

Now we can solve for equilibrium under different scenarios. To start, let's run the following baseline equilibrium: labor tax rate at 25 percent, capital tax rate at 15 percent, and corporate tax rates at 0 percent. First, set the tax rates and exogenous parameters, then calculate the remaining parameters. After doing that, set counterfactual tax rates. Under the baseline scenario, we keep the counterfactual tax rates the same as the baseline tax rates and solve for the equilibrium. Running the model under these specifications gives the expected results, prices of factors and outputs are near unity, and labor supply is close to 60 percent of GDP.

As was discussed earlier, the corporate income tax is very similar to a capital income tax. See Radulescu and Stimmelmayr (2010) for an application to Germany on impacts of corporate tax changes. We can recreate a very similar equilibrium by setting corporate income tax rates to 15 percent and zeroing out capital income taxes. We do this by setting the baseline taxes to the same rate as in the previous example, calibrating the model, and then setting the counterfactual capital income tax rate to 0 percent and the counterfactual corporate income tax rate to 15 percent. Doing so results in a very similar equilibrium as the baseline: prices are near unity, and labor supply is very close to 60 percent of GDP.

In conclusion, the process of solving a model with constant returns to scale production is very similar to our process of solving a model with decreasing returns to scale production. The big difference is that we must use per-unit demand functions because there is no optimal output level as there is with decreasing returns to scale. We then use the consumer's demand for goods and to feed quantities back into the production function and solve for factor demands. Using those factor demands we can calculate excess demands. Once we have excess demands, the rest of the program solves as before, with excess demands returned to the algorithm and a new price vector being generated.

9 Incorporating intermediate inputs

Now that we have discussed how to build a model with the basic factors of production, the next exercise is to add in intermediate production. As discussed, intermediate inputs are goods and services that are used by firms to make another output. In Chapter 8, firms would use capital and labor to make some final output. Now the firm can use factors as well as output from other firms.

9.1 Input-output matrices

In order to add intermediate production, we use input-output (IO) matrix analysis. This uses a matrix that shows how goods flow through an economy. To create an IO matrix, we need to know how much a firm spends on each good it uses as inputs. An IO matrix is constructed by using the columns as sectors, and the rows are the subsequent inputs. For example, we could use the following IO matrix (Figure 9.1).

To read this matrix, start with the first column. This says that the Goods sector directs 30 percent of its total cost on buying output from the Goods sector and 10 percent buying output from the Services sector. Another way to interpret this is to say that for every $1.00 of output from the Goods sector, $0.30 is spent on Goods inputs and $0.10 is spent on Services. Production must also obey Walras' law, so we know that the rest of the expenditure, $0.60, goes to capital and labor factors. Following the logic from Chapter 8, one can solve for output prices by using the following equation:

$$P = VA(P_K, P_L) \times [I - A]^{-1}$$

This equation tells us that to determine output prices, we only need the matrix A and the expenditure on value added $VA(P_K, P_L)$. The matrix A is the IO matrix that we defined previously, so it is a matrix of parameters that is set before the program executes.

	Goods	Services
Goods	0.3	0.15
Services	0.1	0.25

Figure 9.1 Input-output matrix

DOI: 10.4324/9780429295485-9

The other variable, $VA(P_K, P_L)$, is the only variable left that we need to find to determine the vector of prices. The easiest way to set up this problem is by using a "nest" structure found in multiple CGE models. This method breaks down the production function into several nests such that each nest outputs a composite good from multiple inputs. For example, the value-added nest in this model takes in capital and labor and outputs a single value-added composite. The nest works just like a production function in the previous models. For this example, we will keep the same Cobb-Douglas specification from the last several models.

$$k_i^* = \frac{\overline{va_i}}{\gamma_i} \left[\left(\frac{P_K}{P_L} \right) \left(\frac{1-\sigma_i}{\sigma_i} \right) \right]^{\sigma_i - 1}$$

$$l = \frac{\overline{va_i}}{\gamma_i} \left[\left(\frac{P_K}{P_L} \right) \left(\frac{1-\sigma_i}{\sigma_i} \right) \right]^{\sigma_i}$$

In the previous equations, we solve for the demands for labor and capital per unit of output given their respective prices. These two equations take in the parameters σ_i and γ_i that are calibrated to fit the data in the baseline. In addition, we also include the parameter $\overline{va_i}$, which scales the capital and labor demands by the overall share of the value-added composite in production. The production technology can be thought of as using the intermediate and value-added composites in fixed shares. Then, within the value-added composite, the firm can make some substitutions between capital and labor if prices change.

9.2   Intermediate production

Let us look at how to add intermediate production. For this chapter we will be working with the file "intermediate-with-taxes.jl" in the folder "Intermediate." First, we need to define our parameters. The σ_i and γ_i are calibrated the same way as in previous models. Remember, we are calibrating production demands to a single unit of the value-added composite. After calibrating these parameters, we need to specify the IO matrix. We will code this directly in the code, but for most applications, importing these numbers from a data file is best practice.

```
A = [0.3 0.15; 0.1 0.25]
```

We use the variable A to store the IO matrix for our code. The code in the previous section recreates the IO matrix in the preceding table. We take the difference between unity and the sum of the shares in the IO matrix to get the $\overline{va_i}$ share parameter. This can be done easily by using the sum function in Julia. The second argument, dims, tells the sum function to sum over columns.

```
va = 1. - sum(A, dims = 1)
```

These parameters are all defined outside the main loop for our program. We are keeping taxes in this model, so our price vector has three entries, two for the prices of labor and capital and one for the government budget constraint. Beginning the main loop, we call off the vector of prices just as before. The first step is to solve for optimal demands of capital and labor given factor prices.

```
# Manufacturing
capitalDemand[1] = (va[1]/
  gamma[1])*((wage*beta[1])/
(rent * (1 + cIncTax[1]) * alpha[1])) ^ alpha[1]
# Services
capitalDemand[2] = (va[2]/
  gamma[2])*((wage*beta[2])/
(rent * (1 + cIncTax[2]) * alpha[2])) ^ alpha[2]
# Manufacturing
laborDemand[1] = (va[1]/gamma[1])*((rent * (1 +
  cIncTax[1]) * alpha[1])
/(wage*beta[1])) ^ beta[1]
# Services
laborDemand[2] = (va[2]/gamma[2])*((rent * (1 +
  cIncTax[2]) * alpha[2])
/(wage*beta[2])) ^ beta[2]
```

This code is the same as in previous models except that we include the share of value-added in each equation. Remember to allocate the correct shares to each of the industries; in this case, those are services and manufacturing.

The next step is to calculate the expenditure per unit on the value-added composite. This is done by multiplying the factor demands by the costs for each. In the

```
case of labor, this is just the wage per unit. In
the case of capital, this is the rental price and
corporate income taxes.
vamc[1] = wage * laborDemand[1] +
rent * (1 + cIncTax[1]) * capitalDemand[1]
vamc[2] = wage * laborDemand[2] +
rent * (1 + cIncTax[2]) * capitalDemand[2]
```

In the code, *vamc* is the vector of expenditures per unit on the value-added composite for each industry. We combine this with our IO matrix to find output prices given these factor demand quantities. To solve, we simply multiply by the total requirements matrix. Before running the loop, we find the total requirements matrix so that we have a matrix *AINV* that returns the vector of prices when multiplied by the per unit cost of value-added expenditures.

```
AINV = inv(eye(2) - A)
global price = AINV * (vamc)
```

Thus, intermediate production can be modeled without including output prices in the vector of prices we are solving the whole system on. This dimensional reduction allows the program to solve faster because the length of time taken to solve is a function of the number of entries in the main price vector. The simultaneity problem still exists because firms need to know the output prices of all goods before they can solve for input demand quantities. However, because of the linear nature of the inputs in the production function, we can do this by inverting the matrix of Leontief coefficients.

After finding output prices, we calculate the income for the consumer based on the rent and wage, and after finding income, we can calculate consumption using income and output prices.

```
# Calculate consumer demands
global income = rent * (1 - capitalTax) * capital-
  Supply +
wage * (1 - laborTax) * laborSupply + TR
# Demand for goods
x[1] = (theta/(price[1]*(1+salesTax[1]))) * income
# Demand for services
x[2] = ((1-theta)/(price[2]*(1+salesTax[2]))) *
income
```

The vector *x* is the final demands from the household, and we can use that vector to find total production. Note that this is now different than final demand. As shown previously, final demand is the total production with intermediate inputs removed. To find total factor demands, we need to know total production, not just final demand. We can find total production by using the same method we found prices, except we transpose the matrix *A* before finding the inverse.

```
AINVt = inv(eye(2) - A')
global q = AINVt * x
global i = A. * q'
```

So *AINVt* is calculated in the same way as *AINV* except that we transpose the matrix *A* before subtracting it from the identity matrix and taking the inverse. This is taken directly from the solution methods provided in Chapter 8. The two vectors *q* and *id* are final production and intermediate use, respectively. Each vector contains two entries, one for goods and the other for services. The intermediate use vector we do not actually need to make final calculations, but it can be useful to report. If we were concerned with computation time, we could calculate it after running through the loop.

9.3   Factor demands

Finally, we have total production, which can be used to calculate factor demands, just as before (except we did that with final demands). Using the vector of total production, we multiply that by the respective per-unit coefficients (that we calculated earlier to make the marginal costs of value added).

```
# Find total factor quantities demanded
# These are calculated by multiplying our per-unit
# quantities demanded calculated earlier by total
# amounts sold.
totLaborDemand[1] = q[1] * laborDemand[1]
totLaborDemand[2] = q[2] * laborDemand[2]
# Total capital quantity demanded is calculated in
   the same way
totCapitalDemand[1] = q[1] * capitalDemand[1]
totCapitalDemand[2] = q[2] * capitalDemand[2]
```

Now that we have found factor demands, the rest of the program focuses on calculating the excess demands. Taxes are collected on factor income and final demands. And excess demands are constructed for labor, capital, and the government budget balance. The program then loops back and calls off a new vector of prices, and the model runs again until the tolerance is low enough to exit.

Now that we have created a model that has some basic intermediate inputs, we can include intermediate taxes. To include taxes on intermediate inputs, we need to augment the matrix we inverted to determine prices. This is because final output prices will need to include any expenditures on taxes. We start this by defining two tax rates on goods 1 and 2, which are defined as t_1 and t_2, respectively. The augmented direct requirements matrix, defined as *A*, is then defined as follows:

$$\hat{A} = \begin{bmatrix} a_{11}(1+t_1) & a_{12}(1+t_2) \\ a_{21}(1+t_1) & a_{22}(1+t_2) \end{bmatrix}$$

The condition on prices then becomes the following:

$$P = VA + \widehat{A} \times P$$

So now output prices include the markup from taxes on intermediate inputs. This means that the inverse matrix in our code needs to be changed as well. Turning to the program, we change the definition of our variable *AINV* such that it reflects the augmented direct requirements matrix. We first declare a vector of parameters *intTax* that contains the two taxes on intermediate goods. Next, we include the tax rates to augment the inverse matrix *AINV* like so:

```
AINV = inv(eye(2) - A. * (1. + [intTax; intTax]))
```

Last, we need to include the revenue from the tax on intermediate goods in our government revenue. Remember we calculate the matrix of intermediate input consumption as i, so the total revenue from intermediate input taxes is defined as follows:

```
sum(price'. * i. * intTax)
```

With this we can perform some basic policy analysis. In the code there is a section labeled "define tax rates" where we give three scenarios. The first scenario is our baseline equilibrium where capital and labor tax rates are 25 percent, the sales tax rate is 5 percent, and intermediate taxes are zero. First, set the tax rates in the code to scenario one by uncommenting these lines and running the model. Once the model exits, change the tax rate on intermediate goods inputs to 5 percent by uncommenting the lines under scenario two and running the model again. We see that the model predicts that real GDP falls by 1.5 percent, and government revenues increase by 11 percent. Additionally, we see that the price on capital falls by about 2 percent. This follows from the observation that intermediate input taxes reduce the productivity of firms and thus reduce the return to capital.

This technique can be used to solve CGE models with large numbers of sectors without adding length to the price vector, so the model does not increase in computational complexity. This is especially useful when trying to use real-world model data. This method does, however, assume that there is no substitution between intermediation inputs to production, which may not be reasonable for all purposes. The modeler must take these assumptions into account when deriving an analysis from such constructions.

10 Trade, the Armington approach

This chapter goes through an exercise looking at how to add trade to a model using the Armington assumption. Firms and final consumers can purchase goods and services internationally. However, even if goods and services have the same label, they are considered different based on where they are purchased from. This is what is meant by the Armington assumption: goods are differentiated by origin of production. Another model that could be considered is the non-Armington or homogeneous goods model, where goods are the same regardless of origin.

Much of the structure of models constructed in previous exercises will remain the same. To make this exercise easier, we will create two copies of the domestic economies that will be foreign regions the domestic region trades with. Each economy will produce two types of output: goods and services. They can then buy and sell any goods produced by other countries. Goods and services are produced using labor and capital as well as intermediate consumption of goods. Intermediate inputs and capital can be bought from different countries, but all labor is specific to each country. This assumption of immobile labor is common for most CGE models.

We assume there are three regions in this model, these could be countries, states, cities, etc. The model works for any group of legally delineated group of economies that trade amongst themselves. One important addition that must also be made is an outside economy that contains the "rest of the world." This allows the modeler to control where all the trade is going or coming from. Remember, all models expressed here must obey Walras' law, all income must equal expenditure. However, by including multiple smaller economies, we can "zoom in" on specific trade patterns and analyze policies affecting inter-regional trade.

We are keeping much of the structure of previous models. Goods and services are produced using Cobb-Douglas inputs of labor and capital and Leontief inputs of intermediate production. For simplicity, we will skip declaring variables and calibration and come back to it. Instead, we will start inside the loop that solves the model. To start with, we call off the prices that we will need to solve the model. For this model we will need seven prices to be called off. Three wages for each of the regions, three transfers to clear each region, and one worldwide capital price. Next, we do the same thing as when firms use intermediate inputs, except now each firm uses capital from other regions and only local labor. So services produced by any

DOI: 10.4324/9780429295485-10

region uses capital, which it can source from any region, and labor, which it can only source from its local region, to form the value-added component of production. We calculate value-added demands in the same way as the intermediate production model, except we use the global price of capital and the local price of labor.

$$k_i^* = \frac{\overline{va_i}}{\gamma_i} \left[\left(\frac{P_K}{P_L} \right) \left(\frac{1-\sigma_i}{\sigma_i} \right) \right]^{\sigma_i - 1} \tag{E10.1}$$

$$l = \frac{\overline{va_i}}{\gamma_i} \left[\left(\frac{P_K}{P_L} \right) \left(\frac{1-\sigma_i}{\sigma_i} \right) \right]^{\sigma_i} \tag{E10.2}$$

After the per-unit demands for capital and labor are found, we know the marginal cost of value-added components for each firm. We can then use the zero-profit condition to solve for the vector of commodity prices. For this model, we will solve for prices in the same way as the previous model, by simply inverting a matrix. The matrix here will need to include six rows and columns to reflect the goods and services from each region (Table 10.1).

The columns represent each industry's output, and each row is an input to that industry. This is the same input-output matrix as before except we have added goods and services for each region. One can solve for the vector of prices necessary to fulfill the zero-profit condition by solving the equation and inverting the matrix.

We have chosen this model for its simplicity. By using the matrix formulation to solve this model, we are assuming that the trade relationships between countries are linear. Most trade models assume some level of substitution between inputs from different origins. Armington's original model used the constant elasticity of substitution formulation to create some level of substitution between two products. This creates a nested framework where firms decide how to source inputs from different regions based on relative prices in those regions. The present model allows prices to differ between regions, but it does not allow substitution.

Table 10.1 Matrix template of a three-region trade model

	Region 1 Goods	Region 1 Services	Region 2 Goods	Region 2 Services	Region 3 Goods	Region 3 Services
Region 1 Goods						
Region 1 Services						
Region 2 Goods						
Region 2 Services						
Region 3 Goods						
Region 3 Services						

Using the constant elasticity of substitution, a typical combination of inputs from different regions can be expressed as follows:

$$X_i = \left(b_{ij} X_{ij}^{-\rho_i} \right)^{\frac{1}{-\rho_i}} \qquad \text{(E10.3)}$$

Where X_i is the composite of a particular input for production in region i sourced from all regions j. For example, X_i could be total goods purchased by region i, which is a combination of goods region i purchased from all regions j. The demand for goods from each region can then be expressed as a demand function of prices from different regions.

$$X_{ij} = b_{ij}^{\sigma_i} X_i \left(\frac{P_{ij}}{P_i} \right)^{\sigma_i} \qquad \text{(E10.4)}$$

Where σ_i is an elasticity of substitution among regions that goods would originate from. In the trade literature, this is called an Armington elasticity, and it is commonly estimated by studies.

For this model we are assuming an Armington elasticity of zero. Although this approach is inaccurate from the empirical standpoint, it allows to mitigate the complexity associated with computation. If the Armington elasticity is zero, then the problem is linear, and the modeler is only required to invert a matrix. If we kept the substitution elasticity as non-zero and finite, we would need to solve a system of non-linear demand equations. This could be done by adding prices to our initial price vector, or it could be done by using a Newton-type method. These partial equilibrium systems are usually more easily solved compared to general equilibrium systems, so they can be solved in a similar fashion. Instead of multiplying the value-added cost vector by the inverted input-output matrix, we could use a nonlinear zero finding algorithm and return the price vector where price minus marginal cost is zero. This would add some time to the computation of each loop, and that computational cost would need to be weighed against simply adding the commodity prices to the initial price vector.

The code for this section is in the ALLCODE folder, under the subdirectories Julia and Trade. The code is contained in the Julia source file named "Trade.jl." After calculating all commodity prices for all regions, we can move forward with the program. Just as before, we calculate the income received by a region as the sum of earnings from the allocations of capital and labor and any transfers received from the government.

```
income[i] = rent * (1 - capitalTax[i]) *
capitalSupply[i] +
wage[i] * (1 - laborTax[i]) * laborSupply[i] +
TR[i]
```

Each region has a single government budget, and transfers are not made between governments; thus we need multiple prices to clear government budgets in our price vector. We could have also assumed a single government that regulates all regions, in which case we would only need one government budget constraint. There could also be the case that there are multiple government levels. For example, multiple states within a single nation. Each state would have a government that taxes and transfers only within that state and a second level of government that can tax and transfer for all states. This simply comes down to the modeler's preference.

After calculating income, we can then calculate final demands as before using Cobb-Douglas demands. Since we are assuming that the Armington elasticity is zero between different origins of goods or services, we can decompose final demands for imports by simply using Leontief shares.

```
# Demand for goods
xgr[i,j] = impGoods[i,j] *
(theta[i,1]/(prices[j,1] *
(1 + salesTax[i,1] + tariffG[i,j]))) * income[i]
# Demand for services
xsr[i,j] = impServ[i,j] *
(theta[i,2]/(prices[j,2] *
(1 + salesTax[i,2] + tariffS[i,j]))) * income[i]
```

The parameters *impGoods* and *impServ* are vectors of shares of goods and services purchased from each region. For this example, all regions buy 90 percent of goods from domestic sources and 5 percent from each of the other two regions, and they buy 98 percent of their services from domestic sources and 1 percent from each of the other two regions. Some trade models will take the assumption that services are "non-tradeable" with the argument that it is impossible to trade something like a haircut to other regions. However, caution should be exercised since some services, such as customer support, financial services, education services, and even health services, are traded regularly via telecommunication.

After calculating final demands, we can calculate the tax revenue collected for each region. One change here is that since the model incorporates a corporate income tax and a capital income tax, earnings on capital can return revenue to more than one region. For example, suppose a firm opens in region 1 using capital from region 2. Region 1 would have authority to charge the firm a corporate income tax, but region 2 would have authority to charge a capital income tax (since that is where the household that owns the capital resides). This does not change our code, however, since we are just charging the corporate income tax on demand for capital and the capital income tax on the supply of capital. Since labor is not traded between regions, there is no change.

```
cIncTax[i,:]. * rent. * totCapitalDemand[i,:]) + #
Corporate inc. tax rev
capitalTax[i] * rent * capitalSupply[i] + # Capi-
   tal income tax rev
wage[i] * laborTax[i] * laborSupply[i] + # Labor
income tax rev
```

Next to calculate is sales taxes, which are the same for all goods and services purchased in a region regardless of which region they were produced in. As a good for final consumption crosses the border for sale in another region, the consumer pays both a tariff and sales tax on the final price of the good if they exist. Imported intermediate inputs, which will be used for further production, however, only pay the tariff.

```
sum(xgr[i,:]. * prices[:,1] * salesTax[i,1]) + #
Sales tax revenue goods
sum(xsr[i,:]. * prices[:,2] * salesTax[i,2]) + #
Sales tax revenue services
```

A big difference between this model and the previous model is that we are calculating tariffs on imported goods. First, we multiply the vector of final demands and prices by the tariffs rates for each region and country. To calculate tariffs, we store the tariff rates in a matrix where each entry has the rate for the origin and destination region like the input-output matrix we are using. This means that along the diagonal the tariff rates are zero because a region does not charge a tariff on domestic sources. The two matrices *tariffG* and *tariffS* contain the tariff rates for goods and services, respectively.

```
sum(xgr[i,:]. * prices[:,1]. * tariffG[i,:]) + #
Tariff tax revenue goods
sum(xsr[i,:]. * prices[:,2]. * tariffS[i,:]) + #
Tariff tax revenue services
```

We also assume that tariffs are charged on imported intermediate inputs. To add this into our program, we create a matrix of tax rates where each entry is the sum of the tariff and intermediate inputs tax. This allows us to take account of the price distortions when we find the resulting commodity price vector. Additionally, we can find total revenue garnered by intermediate input taxes and tariffs by multiplying the matrix of intermediate input consumption by the matrix of total tax rates on intermediate consumption.

```
sum(sg[j,:]. * (priceV. * Atax[j,:])) + # Taxes on
intermediate inputs
sum(sg[j+1,:]. * (priceV. * Atax[j+1,:])) # Taxes
on intermediate inputs
```

After calculating the total revenue collected through taxation, we can move on to calculating the excess demands vector, which is then fed back into the algorithm to resume the main loop of the program. We have seven prices in our initial vertex, so we also need seven entries in the excess demands vector. The order we have chosen for this program is putting domestic wages for all regions first, followed by a single entry for the global price of capital, and then followed by the three prices to balance government budgets. For the first three entries of the excess demands vector, we simply subtract domestic labor supply from domestic labor demand in each region. A similar exercise is performed for the last three entries, where we subtract total transfers from total revenue collected.

```
# Excess demands
exDem[1] = sum(totLaborDemand[1,:]) - laborSupply[1]
exDem[2] = sum(totLaborDemand[2,:]) - laborSupply[2]
exDem[3] = sum(totLaborDemand[3,:]) - laborSupply[3]
exDem[4] = sum(totCapitalDemand) -
  sum(capitalSupply)
exDem[5] = R[1] - TR[1]
exDem[6] = R[2] - TR[2]
exDem[7] = R[3] - TR[3]
```

The only different calculation is the fourth entry, which is for the excess demand for capital. For this entry, we must remember to sum all capital allocations across all regions and subtract that result from the total sum of all capital demand across regions. We then feed the excess demands vector to the algorithm using *mCalc!* function, which returns the new price vector. The loop exits when the sum of squared excess demands has reached a small enough tolerance.

While we have made some simplifying assumptions in creating a trade model here, this lays out the basic structure one needs to think about when creating an Armington type model. Several other features could be added to the model to increase the usefulness in studying certain situations. Instead of exhausting all possible options, we will point out some basic features of trade between multiple regions that exist due to computational constraints we have imposed on the model. For example, we used the assumption defined in the Armington model that imports are differentiated by the country of their original production. Instead, we could also create a model where exports are differentiated by their shipment destination, or even both. Additionally, we could assume that goods and services have no differentiation based on their origin or destination and essentially assert that goods and services are the same no matter where they were produced or shipped.

11 Taxes and the government

Let us now consider what we have done so far. We have introduced the general equilibrium model and have shown how to find a numerical solution to the problem of finding market clearing prices for certain types of economies. There were essentially two types of such economies, open and closed. What is missing? The answer is that there is no government or public sector. Hence the solution method and underlying model cannot be used for any sort of policy analysis. For example, suppose that we wish to carry out the welfare analysis of a tax increase. Such analysis would be impossible since there are no taxes in the model due to not having a government to collect or distribute tax revenues. Thus, our model, as it now stands, would be useful only for studying a static economy without policy changes. So what is the problem with introducing a government accompanied by all the things that governments do: tax, spend, subsidize, and many other public policies? The next section will begin to address this problem in the simplest possible case.

The basic case: let us introduce the most basic possible government. This government does only two things: it collects taxes, and it spends its revenues by making lump sum transfers to consumers. By this we mean that there is a system of revenue transfers that is independent of what people do. For example, each person receives an equal share of government revenues. Another example might be that people born in an odd number year receive one amount, while people born in an even year receive a different amount. In short, nothing that a person does impacts the transfer he receives. In addition, there is a balanced budget constraint so that there is no public borrowing and hence no requirement for debt financing. Let us now introduce taxes.

There are two types of taxes. The first is a direct tax levied on factor inputs. The most basic factor inputs are capital and labor.[1] Hence total direct taxes, T_D, are given by the following:

$$T_D = t_K P_K y_K + t_L P_L y_L \tag{E11.1}$$

Here t_K is the rate of taxation of capital, that is, the corporate income tax. P_K is the rental price of capital, while y_K is the input of capital. Similarly, t_L is the

DOI: 10.4324/9780429295485-11

wage tax rate, that is, the tax on income accruing to labor. P_L is the wage rate, and y_L represents inputs of labor. We interpret these taxes as a corporate profit tax and a personal income tax, that is, a tax on wage income that is withheld at the source.

Total indirect taxes, T_C, where the tax (sales tax) rate on good j is given by t_{Cj}, are estimated by the following:

$$T_c = \sum_1^N t_{Cj} P_j x_j \tag{E11.2}$$

Where x_j is the consumption, and P_j is the price of good j, respectively. Thus, this tax is levied at the point of sale, as is typical in the US. We could also introduce many other forms of a consumption tax, such as a value-added tax (VAT), which is commonly used in much of the world outside the USA.

We can now add the different sources of taxation together to get total tax revenues. Total tax revenues, T, are given by the following:

$$T = T_D + T_C \tag{E11.3}$$

Suppose that tax revenues are paid out as transfer payments to consumers. Consumer i receives a transfer payment TR_i where

$$\sum_{i=1}^M TR_i = T \tag{E11.4}$$

11.1   The simultaneity problem between taxes and transfers

We face a simultaneity problem. Recall that in the case of the simple economy with no government, each consumer could solve his utility optimization problem by knowing the prices in the market, as well as their individual budget constraint. The budget constraint is, in turn, dependent upon the consumer's holding of factors. The consumer has private information on these holdings, while market prices are public information. Now, however, in order for each consumer to know their individual budget constraint, they need not only to know the prices they face, but they need also to know their individual transfer payment TR_i. These transfers depend upon the government's tax collection.

Here is our simultaneity problem. In order for these aggregate tax collections to be calculated, we need to know TR_i, which in turn depends upon individual consumption decisions. Hence there is a problem. The individual consumer cannot optimize until he knows his budget constraint. However, he does not know his budget constraint until he knows his transfer payments. But these payments depend upon tax payments made by everyone else. Thus, we have a situation in which my consumption depends upon the consumption, and hence tax payments, of other people.

11.2   The introduction of a tax proxy

We now face an unfamiliar situation in basic microeconomics: each individual's consumption decision depends upon choices made by other people. How are we to deal with this? This problem is solved by introducing a new "price," R, which will be a proxy for the total value of transfer payments. For now, this is an imaginary number. Each consumer will receive a share β_i of this transfer proxy. This share β_i is arbitrary so long as $\sum \beta_i = 1$.

Thus, the consumer's augmented income is given by the following:

$$\check{I}(P) = I(P) + \beta_i(R)$$

11.3   The solution of the model with an extra dimension for taxes

Our extended concept of an equilibrium will be to find a "price," R, such that

$$R = TR$$

Thereby, the transfers made to consumers actually equal the transfers consumers think they will receive. Intuitively, each consumer behaves as if he receives $\beta_i(R)$. The market then generates an equilibrium in which all markets for goods and services clear. Also, at this equilibrium, the amount of taxes collected and transferred to consumers is exactly the amount they thought they would receive. We will not go into the details of the enhanced computation technique but will note that it essentially involves the expansion of the price simplex to one additional dimension, denoting the tax variable.[2]

We can now have any number of goods, any number of consumers, many different types of taxes, as well as different rates within a tax type, yet we only need to solve for factor prices and the tax proxy. Indeed, the addition of the extended price simplex can be broadened to include non-balanced budgets that are financed by public borrowing and monetization. We will cover this topic in a later chapter.

11.4   The possible generalization of the tax proxy concept to other applications

How has the subject progressed over time? The original CGE paper, Shoven and Whalley (1972),[3] was motivated by Harberger's (1962) paper on the incidence of the corporate income tax in the US.[4] Harberger considered a fundamental question in tax policy: namely, who bears the burden of a particular tax? In order to answer this question, we need to carry out a set of model simulations. First, we need a structural model whose endogenous outcomes represent the outcomes of a real (or possibly hypothetical) economy. Suppose we could simulate our model without taxes. The resulting outcomes would then represent the endogenous outcomes of a "tax free" economy. The hypothetical question is then what the outcomes would be if a new tax regime was added. By comparing the taxed and non-taxed economies, welfare comparisons could be made. For example, we could look at disaggregated household and see who has done better under the new tax regime and who has done worse.

The Harberger approach was to consider localized changes in the original equilibrium that might be caused by tax rate changes. This methodology was reasonable for small changes. However, the intended experiment was to replace the entire US corporate income tax structure by something completely different. For such an experiment one really needs a global general equilibrium methodology approach since the proposed changes cannot be localized. This is what the Shoven and Whalley paper did. That is, use a CGE model in which changes do not need to be small and localized.

At about the same time as the Shoven and Whalley work, Miller and Spencer (1977) constructed a CGE model to analyze the UK's joining the common market. This topic, that is, the impact of joining the common market, is another example of a counterfactual tax simulation. The base case would be the UK prior to joining. That is, the UK with all the tariffs on imports that existed prior to liberalization. The counterfactual case would be a simulation in which tariffs are imposed. These tariffs are mechanically the same as taxes. The difference is that they are levied upon imports, not upon domestically produced goods. These papers indicate the general direction the field has followed ever since: generate a calibration benchmark simulation. Then carry out counterfactual simulations that represent different public policies.

An example

There are, of course, many papers that use CGE methodology to analyze tax policies. Here is an example of one such approach.[5] This paper was motivated by a very much real-world situation. In the paper we construct a dynamic model of the Australian economy that has a regional subsection representing Western Australia. Within the West Australia sub-economy, there is a separate technology for the gold mining industry. We implement the model and simulate a 2.5 percent tax on gold exports. The outcome shows no fiscal improvement at the national level, although the West Australian budget improves slightly. Real income falls both nationally and in West Australia as the trade balance deteriorates, and an increased real interest rate causes investment to fall. We conclude that the taxation of gold exports leads to few measurable benefits.

The situation at the time this paper was written was that gold output had been growing strongly in Australia in recent years. Production of gold in Western Australia (WA) rose by 4.7 percent in 1994. This represented about 74 percent of total Australian gold production and about 8 percent of total world output. Indeed, only South Africa and the US produced more gold than Australia in 1994. Gold had become especially important for the WA economy, and its current output value of Australian 3257 million made it Western Australia's highest-valued mineral product. Almost 90 percent of Western Australia's gold output was (and is) exported, with the main importers being Japan and Singapore.

The WA government in the 1990s was considering enforcing a state royalty on gold production, primarily as a source of revenues. In particular, a 2.5 percent tax was proposed. Gold was currently exempted from any such royalty. The most common rationale for this tax was that like all other minerals, gold mining should pay a fee for the purchase of the ore from the State. Another reason was the belief that the tax would have little, if any, economic effects. In other words, the supply elasticity of gold is relatively low. In addition, almost all demand for Australian gold is foreign, so the thinking was that foreigners would bear any burden from the tax. Given the importance of gold to the WA economy, and to Australia as a whole, the imposition of a tax on gold should be carefully examined.

We thus have a comparison of tax policies. In particular, what would the implications of the proposed gold tax be? We construct a model that uses two discrete time periods with perfect foresight. That is, all future prices are correctly anticipated. There is production technology at both the state, WA, and national level, RA (rest of Australia). There are also capital and labor that are specific to the two parts of the country.

There are two governments, representing RA and WA. The RA government collects taxes and import duties and pays for the production of public goods and subsidies. Also, the RA government covers both domestic and foreign interest obligations on public debt. The WA government spends on local infrastructure but, unlike the federal government, receives only a portion of the taxes generated locally since most tax collection is done by the federal government. We model the WA government as receiving all its revenues from revenue sharing from the federal government. The WA government finances a deficit solely by domestic borrowing, rather than by the additional instruments of monetization and foreign borrowing. Accordingly, a WA deficit leads to debt, rather than monetary expansion.

Gold exports are determined separately. We take supply elasticities from Selvanathan and Selvanathan (1998)[6] and use them to derive export response. We use Selvanathans' one-year dynamic elasticity estimates to derive a medium-term supply response elasticity. Thus, the export response of WA gold is endogenously determined based on the domestic currency price change and the assumed supply elasticities (p. 309). Demand for imports is endogenous; foreign lending is exogenous. Thus, gross capital inflows are exogenous, but the overall change in reserves is endogenous.

Having developed this model, we used Australian data to implement and calibrate a numerical version of it. By this we mean that we run our model using the Australian parameters that we have estimated. We then want to see how well the simulated outcomes of the model approximate the actual endogenous outcomes of the economy. Table 11.1 gives the simulated outcomes of the main macroeconomic variables for both the WA economy as well as the RA economy.

We accurately project the growth rate of real GDP. However, we underestimate tax revenues. This discrepancy is due to our inclusion of only a limited number of taxes. Our simulated values for the tax revenues of the RA government and for the WA State income are reasonably accurate. We are also precise in simulating the national rate of inflation. Our prediction of national exports is on target, although imports are low. Interest rates are reasonably accurately predicted.

We now would like to see what our model says about imposing a tax on gold. Suppose we now impose a tax on the exports of gold. We will introduce a 2.5 percent tax on gold paid by producers. The results of this simulation are given in Tables 11.2 and 11.3.

Table 11.1 Base simulation*

	1990-1991		1991-1992	
Nominal GDP (a)	378.1	(378.1)	407.2	(384.7)
Real GDP (b)	257.1	(257.1)	257.1	(257.9)
Government spending (c)	24.5	(27.2)	25.8	(28.5)
Revenues (c)	16.7	(24.7)	20.3	(24.7)
Government budget surplus (c)	−7.8	(−2.5)	−5.5	(−3.8)
WA state income (a)	40.7	(34.3)	41.6	(36.7)
RA/WA migration (percent) (d)	na		0.2	
WA gold output (gross) (e)	100	(na)	104.9	(na)
WA budget surplus (f)	4.5	(na)	9.6	(na)
Exports (c)	13.4	(13.8)	13.2	(14.3)
Imports (c)	9.1	(13.0)	11.2	(13.3)
Trade balance (c)	4.3	(0.8)	2.0	(1.0)
Inflation rate (g)	8.1	(8.1)	7.7	(5.2)
Interest rate (g, h)	11.2	(11.2)	10.1	(8.9)
Real interest rate (g)	2.8	(2.8)	2.2	(3.5)

*The numbers in parenthesis are historical values
(a) – In billions of dollars; (b) – in billions of 1984/85 dollars; (c) – as a percent of GDP; (d) – as a percent of the RA workforce that moves to WA after the first year; A (-) sign indicates migration from WA to RA; (e) – an index number based on 1990/91; (f) – as a percent of WA state income; (g) – percent; (h) – The historical interest rate is the ten-year Treasury bond rate, taken from *Reserve Bank of Australia Bulletin* (December 1992), Table F2.

Table 11.2 A 2.5 percent tax on gold (columns refer to the same years as in Table 11.1)

Nominal GDP (a)	377.3	405.8
Real GDP (b)	257.1	256.9
Government spending (c)	24.4	25.8
Revenues (c)	16.6	20.3
Government budget surplus (c)	−7.8	−55
WA state income (a)	40.6	41.4
RA/WA migration (percent) (d)	NA	0.2
WA gold output (gross) (e)	99.5	103.7
WA budget surplus (f)	4.6	9.7
Exports (c)	13.3	13.2
Imports (c)	9.1	11.3
Trade balance (c)	4.2	1.9
Inflation rate (g)	7.9	7.6
Interest rate (g)	11.1	10.1
Real interest rate (g)	3	2.3

(a) – In billions of dollars; (b) – in billions of 1984/85 dollars; (c) – as a percent of GDP; (d) – as a percent of the RA workforce that moves to WA after the first year; A (-) sign indicates migration from WA to RA; (e) – an index number based on 1990/91; (f) – as a percent of WA state income; (g) – percent.

The observed changes are compelling. Thus, real national income declined by 0.08 percent by the second year, as compared with the benchmark case. The government budget deficit remained roughly constant in both years. WA State income declined, along with moderate drops in gold output of 0.5 percent in the first year

Table 11.3 Percentage changes caused by tax implementation (g)

Nominal GDP (a)	−0.2	−0.3
Real GDP (b)	0.0	−0.08
Government spending (c)	−0.4	0.0
Revenues (c)	−0.6	0.0
Government budget surplus (c)	0.0	0.0
WA state income (a)	−0.2	−0.5
RA/WA migration (percent) (d)	NA	0.0
WA gold output (gross) (e)	−0.5	−1.1
WA budget surplus (f)	2.2	1.0
Exports (c)	−0.7	0.0
Imports (c)	0.0	0.9
Trade balance (c)	−2.3	−0.5
Inflation rate (g)	−2.5	−1.3
Interest rate (g)	−0.9	0.0
Real interest rate (g)	7.1	4.5

(a) – In billions of dollars; (b) – in billions of 1984/85 dollars; (c) – as a percent of GDP; (d) – the percent of the RA workforce that moves to WA after the first year; A (-) sign indicates migration from WA to RA; (e) – an index number based on 1990/91 of the Table 11.1 simulation; (f) – as a percent of the WA state income; (g) – percent.

Table 11.4 Sectoral Changes Caused by 2.5 Percent Tax on Gold*

Western Australia (WA)

Sectors #	*1990–1991*	*1991–1992*
1 Agriculture	−0.1	−0.1
2 Mining	−0.1	−0.2
3 Manufacturing	−0.1	−0.1
4 Electricity	0.0	−0.1
5 Construction	−0.2	0.0
6 Commerce and Services	−0.1	−0.1
7 Imports from RA	−0.1	−0.1

* These represent the percentage change in real gross output of each of the seven WA production sectors when the gold tax is implemented.

and 1.1 percent by the second year. The trade balance deteriorated by 0.1 percent of GDP in both years, compared with the base case. The WA budget surplus increased.

Table 11.3 presents the results of Table 11.2 in a slightly different fashion. Here we calculate the percentage change in the relevant variable from the base simulation to the simulation with a tax increase.

As a further analysis of our results, Table 11.4 reports percentage changes in gross real output for each of the WA sectors, when Table 11.2 is compared with Table 11.1. Thereby, this gives a disaggregated view of the impact of the tax increase on the real state economy.

The tax change had a small and relatively uniform effect upon sectoral output in WA. Sectoral changes were largely generated by changes in factor prices, which were, in turn, uniform across sectors. Accordingly, the only sectoral differences came from the different structure of costs. Imports from RA declined because of the slight decline in the WA State income. We also observed that WA sectoral gross (real) outputs declined less than did WA nominal income, as shown in Table 11.3. The reason for this is that the WA rate of inflation declined as a result of the tax change, just as the RA inflation rate. Accordingly, the decline in nominal WA income was greater than the real decline, which would essentially correspond to the sectoral changes of Table 11.4.

We thus see that the gold tax had a slight but largely negative impact upon both the national and WA economies. Indeed, the expected national budgetary improvements did not materialize, while RA and WA real incomes declined. Moreover, real interest rates increased, and the trade balance deteriorated.

Notes

1 There can be many other types of factor inputs. For example, land is often considered to be a scarce factor. Also there could be many categories of labor, such as skilled and unskilled, farm, non-farm, etc.
2 See, Shoven, J. B., 1974. A Proof of the Existence of a General Equilibrium with Ad Valorem Commodity Taxes. *Journal of Economic Theory*, 8, 1–25.
3 Shoven, J. B., J. Whalley. 1972. A General Equilibrium Calculation of the Effects of Differential Taxation of Income from Capital in the U.S. *Journal of Public Economics*, 1 (3–4), 281–321.
4 See Harberger, A. C. 1962. The Incidence of the Corporation Income Tax. *Journal of Political Economy*, 70 (3), 215–240, June.
5 See Feltenstein, A. 1997. An Analysis of the Implications for the Gold Mining Industry of Alternative Tax Policies: A Regional Disaggregated Model for Australia. *Economic Record*, 73 (223), 305–314.
6 Selvanathan, S., E. A. Selvanathan. 1998. *An Econometric Study of Gold Production and Prices*. Department of Economics, University of Western Australia, Discussion Paper# 98.02, August.

12 Social accounting matrices (SAM) and the construction of a CGE model

12.1 Introduction and definitions

In the construction of a CGE model, using real-world data, possibly the most important data source is a social accounting matrix (SAM). The SAM is, ideally, a spreadsheet rendering of the circular flow of income in a country. It contains the disaggregated production technology, the structure of consumer demand on the basis of representative agents, and international trade flows. These SAMs are available for almost all middle and higher income countries, and they are also available for many less-developed countries. However, the structure and coverage of a particular country-specific SAM may not correspond exactly to what we need in our country application. We may need different data, or we may be trying to implement a theoretical model that does not correspond exactly to the data structure in the SAM.

Thus, what is a SAM? We need a formal definition. Let us quote from Mainar-Causapé et al. (2018).[1]

"A Social Accounting Matrix (SAM) is a comprehensive and economy-wide database recording data about all transactions between economic agents in a specific economy for a specific period of time. A SAM extends the classical Input-Output framework, including the complete circular flow of income in the economy. SAMs interest is twofold: they are the standard database for most whole economy modelers as they provide data for economic modeling (multi-sectorial linear models or the more complex Computable General Equilibrium –CGE- Models) and they show a complete but intuitive snapshot of the economy at hand.

Institutions (households, government, etc.) own factor services and transfer (selling or renting) them in factor markets to activities (producers, industries, etc.). Activities employ factors paying an amount, generating flows of incomes to the institutions. Then, institutions use these incomes to acquire final commodities (goods and services) produced by the activities. The activities collect part of their income from the sale of final commodities to institutions; the rest comes from the sale to other activities as intermediate commodities on the product markets. Hence, a circular flow is generated between institutions and activities linked via factors and product markets.

DOI: 10.4324/9780429295485-12

Besides, institutions can transfer their factor services to domestic or foreign (rest of the world) activities, while activities can hire factor services from domestic or foreign institutions. Similarly, domestic institutions can buy final commodities from domestic or foreign activities, while domestic activities can buy intermediate commodities from domestic or foreign activities. Thus, flows recorded in a SAM include all transaction: purchasing of intermediate goods, hiring of factors, current account transactions of institutions (transfers, consumption expenditure, savings and investments, and any foreign transaction, including direct investment and international trade).

The estimation of a SAM contributes to the study of any economic system since it collects in detail all economic transactions. Its value as a database is enormous, both in the direct application of multi-sector linear models (multipliers) and for the calibration of CGE models. It is also flexible in its structure and in its geographical area (national, regional, multiregional, etc.) and time frame, allowing its use in the analysis of a multitude of economic issues.

A SAM provides an appropriate database for the analysis of the key socio-economic issues such as employment, poverty, growth and income distribution, trade, etc. By the integration of data on households' behavior in National Accounts, a SAM captures macro transactions of an economic system based on micro level transfers between all agents in the economy (Pyatt and Round, 1985; Reinert and Roland-Holst, 1997). It can incorporate various dimensions that are descriptive of the income distribution by disaggregating the households using socio-economic characteristics (e.g., income level, rural-urban division, etc.).

Typically, a social accounting matrix has six basic groups of accounts:

1. Activities and/or commodities
2. (Production) Factors
3. (Private) Institutions – households and corporations/enterprises
4. Government (public institution)
5. (Combined) Capital accounts
6. Accounts for the rest of the world

The final dimension of the matrix is determined by the level of disaggregation of these six basic groups."

12.2   An example of a sophisticated SAM: the case of Pakistan

What does this mean in practice? Rather than describing further theory to introduce SAMs, we will use a specific example. This is the case of Pakistan, a developing country that has a highly detailed data set covering all real, fiscal, and monetary aspects of the economy. In particular, Pakistan has a complete SAM, as well as a corresponding IO matrix for 2007–2008, which are presented in Debowicz et al. (2013).[2] The four relevant excel file Tables 12.1-12.4 can be downloaded from the publisher's website. Let us go through the list of items and examine the corresponding tables in the Pakistan SAM. The first item in the list, "Activities and/or commodities," is given in Table 12.1. Here, in column A, we have the 50 sectoral items in the list of Pakistan activities. The subcategories correspond to national income accounts, agriculture, mining, manufacturing, and so forth. At the same time, there are many individual items that are specific to Pakistan, for example, basmati rice. By this we mean that we would not have this subcategory if, say, we were working on Korea. This indicates that it is important for the researcher to look at the country-specific elements of the SAM, rather than treating all such matrices as if they were standardized.

The next column in the matrix, Factors (only disaggregated ones), shows the factors of production that are used in the Pakistan production technology. Here we notice that there are many more factor categories than in the usual textbook example of capital, labor, and possibly land. We have sector-specific capital, and this capital is immobile over a single period. These categories of capital are different from country to country. In the case of Pakistan, they are as follows:

Capital livestock
Capital other agriculture
Capital formal
Capital informal

How should these capital types be interpreted? A large part of the economy of Pakistan is in agriculture, and it is divided into livestock and other types of agriculture, and each type has its own distinct capital. The other two types of capital listed previously reflect capital used in the urban parts of the country, primarily in manufacturing. This part of the economy is divided between formal and informal sectors. The informal sector is essentially defined as consisting of those firms that do not have registered identities with the tax authorities and hence evade their tax obligations. Clearly this type of disaggregation of capital types would not be suitable for a country with a small agricultural sector or with little or no informal firms.

Let us now look at the ten types of labor, another classification of scarce factors. Here the differentiation between factors is quite different than with capital. There is, first, a distinction between agricultural labor and nonagricultural labor. This distinction is then further refined by the geographical location of the labor; for example, by in which provinces it is located, Sindh, Punjab, or other parts of Pakistan. In addition, it also shows whether the labor is employed in large, medium, or small enterprises registered in those geographic locations. Nonagricultural labor is differentiated, not by location, but by skilled or non-skilled capabilities. These distinctions mean that, in the short run at least, there is no mobility of labor categories. Also, there is no possibility of labor changing its skill category. Again, this categorization of factors would be very different in other countries.

Now let us focus on 12 types of land. There is a distinction among three geographic areas, that is, Sindh, Punjab, and other parts of Pakistan. The land is further subcategorized based on its size, which include large, medium, and small. Medium and small-sized areas are also subdivided into irrigated and non-irrigated parcels of land.

Finally, we have another very important category, households. We see in Table 12.1 that there are 21 households. Of these, there are 15 agricultural household categories, 3 are rural non-farm categories (shopkeepers, mechanics, and others), while 3 are urban groups, categorized by their income levels. From these groups we will obtain the demand functions for the 21 representative consumer types in the economy of Pakistan. Let us turn to Table 12.2.

In Table 12.2 we see the shares of income spent by each representative household category on each type of good.[3] Thus, the first column represents the consumption pattern of the first quintal of urban consumers. We see that they spend 0.25 percent of their income on fruits/vegetables (row 18). Row 54 (total) of course sums to 100. This table is extraordinarily useful to us as we parameterize a CGE model of the country. In particular, these coefficients can be the exponents in a Cobb-Douglas utility function for the consumer category represented by the first urban quintile. Recall that a Cobb-Douglas utility function has the following form:

$$U(x) = x_1^{\alpha_1} x_2^{\alpha_2} \ldots$$

Where $\sum_i \alpha_i = 1$

where x_i is consumption of good i. Thus, by simply taking the data from the SAM, we have the structure of demand, assuming that consumers do have Cobb-Douglas utility functions.

We are now able to parameterize the utility functions of the different consumers (really consumer categories). Thus, we can immediately derive the form of the consumer demand function. However, we are still not able to derive the actual amounts of goods the consumer demands. One important component remains undetermined in forming the consumer side of the economy. This is the source of income. That is, what is the initial ownership of assets of each consumer group? If we look at Table 12.3, Household Income Matrix for Pakistan 2007–2008, we see in the left column the listing of households. The first row gives the types of income from labor, land, and other factors. As a side note, income is a flow, not a stock. However, there is a way around this. If we define one unit of each factor as that which earns one Pakistani Rupee of income, then we immediately have a numerical value for factor endowments. We therefore have the budget constraints for consumers in the initial year. We can therefore specify the consumers' maximization problems and solve for their price-dependent demands. Thus, we now have the numerical structure of demand.

12.3   The first step: extraction of an IO matrix from the SAM

Lastly, we can now look at the production side of the economy. Here we have another example of how useful the SAM is in saving us work gathering data and estimating parameters. Table 12.4 gives the basic structure of the input-output matrix. Each column represents a production activity. The rows represent the inputs of commodities into each production activity. That is, each column produces one good and uses inputs from the other N-1 goods. If we normalize each of these row entries by the total given in the final row, then we have the Leontief coefficients in the IO matrix.

An additional element needs to be added to complete the structure of production. In any input-output matrix, each production activity, that is, column, requires a linear menu of intermediate inputs in order to produce output. These activities also require inputs of scarce factors. Typically, those are given as labor, capital, and land. If we again look at Table 12.4, rows 56–59, we see inputs of urban and rural labor capital and land. One could take these as fixed shares of factor inputs in the production of value added in each activity, but we prefer to assume that there is factor substitution in production of value added. Thus, we will take the shares of these four factors in value added as being the Cobb-Douglas shares in the production of value added. We may thus think of production as being an input-output matrix "sitting on top" of production of value-added functions.

There are, of course, other items to be added in the parameterization of our model, but this gives the basic idea. It should also clarify just how useful the SAM for a country can be in setting up the basic structure of a CGE model of the country. In the particular case of Pakistan, we have an amazingly detailed matrix, SAM-WALK 2010, which gives data on a number of different areas. Such information is available for many, if not most, countries, greatly reducing the data gathering and estimation work for the researcher.

Notes

1 Mainar-Causapé, A. J., E. Ferrari, S. McDonald. 2018. *Social Accounting Matrices: Basic Aspects and Main Steps for Estimation.* European Commission, JRC Technical Report.
2 Debowicz, D., P. Dorosh, H. Haider, S. Robinson. 2013. A Disaggregated and Macro-Consistent Social Accounting Matrix for Pakistan. *Journal of Economic Structures*, 2, 4. <http://dx.doi.org/10.1186/2193-2409-2-4>
3 Three categories are not included for various statistical reasons.

13 Dynamic CGE models with financial assets

We have now covered a number of topics in both the theory and policy implications of CGE models. Just to review, we introduced a basic exchange economy and showed how to use an iterative methodology to derive a price vector that generates a market equilibrium. We then extended the model to include production, first with decreasing returns to scale and then with constant returns to scale (CRS). This was an important addition since most real-world production data is CRS. We then noted that there was no role for public policy at this point since the model lacked basic government policy instruments, taxes, and expenditures. We then brought in taxes on goods and services and maintained Walras' law by having all tax revenues paid out as lump sum transfers to consumers.

13.1 Introduction

Why do we need a time dimension? What is still missing from the model if we wish to come close to the real world? First, we must eliminate the requirement of a balanced budget since countries do, in fact, run budget deficits. The mechanism of lump sum taxes that we introduced is not satisfactory since no such taxes actually exist in any real countries. Thereby, what is the problem if we no longer constrain budget deficits to be zero? The first problem is that we will not maintain Walras' law since the value of demand will be greater than the value of supply. How to solve this problem?

Let us think from the point of view of a macroeconomist who would say that a new approach is needed. Namely, we have to think about how governments actually finance budget deficits. Deficits are financed through the borrowing by Treasuries (in many countries, the Ministry of Finance). More specifically in the context of our model, the Treasury (a new agency in the model) issues bonds that are a promise to repay a loan to the public sector. The supply of bonds will create a supply of financial assets, which are costless to produce. However, why should there be a demand for the bonds? That is, why in a static world would there be any demand for an asset that pays off in the future? That is, one purchases the bond today, but the interest payments on the bond begin to accrue in the future. Clearly this is not possible in a single period model. Hence, we need to introduce the notion of a multi-period model with forward-looking agents. That is, we need to have

DOI: 10.4324/9780429295485-13

consumers who consume today but also save in order to finance their consumption in the future. We also need to have producers who think about the future. More particularly, they produce today to supply consumption by current consumers. In addition, they must invest in new capacity (capital) to meet anticipated future demand, as well as to compensate for the depreciation of capital over time.

Let us now introduce a very simple discrete time intertemporal model that lends itself to CGE implementation. There are N time periods. This is a random number, which can be made essentially as large as we like. For example, if we wish to study long-term effects of a policy change, then n could be 10–20 periods, for example. We are only limited by the speed of our computer. Let us begin by considering the behavior of the consumer in our dynamic world.

13.2 Perfect foresight models

We suppose that all agents optimize in each period over a two-period time horizon with perfect foresight for those two periods. By this we mean that each agent (consumer) knows all prices in both periods simultaneously. This will turn out to be an equilibrium condition, in that at equilibrium each consumer's expectations of future prices are fulfilled, and the expected prices are the actual equilibrium prices. Let us now be a bit more formal.

In period t the consumer optimizes given prices for periods t and $t+1$, combined with expectations for prices for the future after $t+1$. That is, the consumer has complete knowledge of prices in this period and the next, while the future after next period remains foggy. However, the consumer does need to develop a mechanism for generating expectations for the future since his savings decisions will depend upon such expectations. When period $t+2$ arrives, the agent re-optimizes for period $t+2$ and $t+3$, based on new information about period $t+2$ and expectations about the future after period $t+3$.

13.3 Partial perfect foresight: short run perfect foresight with adaptive updating for the long run

Expectations beyond the two-period perfect foresight future are based upon an adaptive mechanism. That is, the consumer looks at the past series of price changes and takes a weighted average of those changes to forecast prices in the next period.[1] Why do we use this combination of perfect foresight and adaptive expectations? If the consumer did not optimize for the entire future of the model, then we would have a situation in which he is myopic about the future after a few periods going forward but then wakes up and finds himself in a new present and must optimize again. On the other hand, we could have perfect foresight for the entire n periods of the model. The main problem with this approach is that the implementation of the actual model numerically produces the multi-period perfect foresight generating highly unstable equilibria. The problem is that a small change far in the future, since perfectly anticipated in the present, will generate a large current change in behavior to compensate for the distant future. Such a large change is correct in a mechanical model, but it is not satisfactory if we are attempting to replicate the behavior of a real economy.

13.4 The consumer's problem

What, specifically, is the problem then? Consumers maximize intertemporal utility functions, which have as arguments the levels of consumption, including imports, and leisure in each of the two perfect foresight periods. Formally, the consumer's problem is then given by the following equation:[2]

$$\text{Max } U(x), \quad x = (x_1, x_{Lu1}, x_{Lr1}, x_2, x_{Lu2}, x_{Lr2}) \tag{E 13.1}$$

Such that

$$(1+t_i)P_i x_i + P_{Lui} x_{Lui} + p_{Lri} x_{Lri} + P_{Mi} x_{Mi} + P_{Bi} x_{Bi} + e_i P_{Bfi} x_{Bfi} = C_i \tag{E13.1a}$$

$$P_{K1} K_0 + P_{A1} A_0 + P_{Lu1} L_{u1} + P_{Lr1} L_{r1} + P_{M1} M_0 + r_0 B_0 + P_{B1} B_0 + e_1 P_{BF1} B_{F0} + TR_1 = N_1$$

$$P_{K2}(1-\delta)K_0 + P_{A2} A_0 + P_{Lu2} L_{u2} + P_{Lr2} L_{r2} + P_{M2} x_{M1} + r_1 x_{B1} + e_2 P_{BF2} x_{BF1} + TR_2 = N_2$$

$$C_i = N_i$$

$$\log P_{Bi} x_{Bi} - \log e_i P_{BFi} x_{BFi} = \alpha + \beta(\log r_i - \log \frac{e_{i+1}}{e_i} r_{Fi}) \tag{E13.1b}$$

$$\log(L_{ui} / L_{ri}) = a_1 + a_2 \log \frac{P_{Lui} - P_{Lri}}{P_{Lui} + P_{Lri}} \tag{E13.1c}$$

$$\log P_{Mi} x_{Mi} = a + b \log(1+t_i)P_i x_i \tag{E13.1d}$$

$$P_{B2} x_{B2} = d_0 + d_1(1+t_2)P_2 x_2 + d_2 \left[\frac{r_2 - \pi_2}{1 + \pi_2} \right] \tag{E13.1e}$$

Where
P_i = price vector of consumption goods in period i.
x_i = vector of consumption in period i. This includes final demand consumption of imports.
C_i = value of aggregate consumption in period i (including purchases of financial assets).
N_i = aggregate income in period i (including potential income from the sale of real and financial assets).
t_i = vector of value-added tax rates in period i.
P_{Lui} = price of urban labor in period i.
L_{ui} = allocation of total labor to urban labor in period i.

x_{Lui} = demand for urban leisure in period i.
P_{Lri} = price of rural labor in period i.
L_{ri} = allocation of total labor to rural labor in period i.
x_{Lri} = demand for rural leisure in period i.
a_2 = elasticity of rural/urban migration.
P_{Ki} = price of capital in period i.
K_0 = initial holding of capital.
P_{Ai} = price of land in period i.
A_0 = initial holding of land.
δ = rate of depreciation of capital.
P_{Mi} = price of money in period i. Money in period 1 is the numeraire.
x_{Mi} = holdings of money in period i.
P_{Bi} = discount price of a certificate of deposit in period i.
π_i = domestic rate of inflation in period i.
r_i, r_{Fi} = the domestic and foreign interest rates in period i.
x_{Bi} = quantity of bank deposits, that is, CDs in period i.
e_i = the exchange rate in terms of units of domestic currency per unit of foreign currency in period i.
x_{BFi} = quantity of foreign currency held in period i.
TR_i = transfer payments from the government in period i.
a, b, α, β = estimated constants.
d_i = constants estimated from model simulations.

Thus, the consumer makes an intertemporal utility-maximizing decision on consumption of goods and services over time. He carries out savings by purchasing bonds, while he holds money because of a cash in advance constraint. Let us now turn to the other side of the real economy, production. Just what constitutes the dynamic element in production? Just as the consumer saves, the producer invests in order to maximize the expected present value of earnings over time. In order to do so, the producer has expectations of future prices with perfect foresight for two periods and adaptive expectations for the future thereafter. Let us now turn to the mechanical formulation of the problem.

13.5   Production and financial assets

There are eight factors of production and three types of financial assets (Table 13.1).

Table 13.1 Production

Factors of production:	Financial assets:
1–5. Capital types	9. Domestic currency
6. Urban labor	10. Bank deposits
7. Rural labor	11. Foreign currency
8. Land	

An input-output matrix, A_t, is used to determine intermediate and final production in period t.

Let y_{Ki}^j, y_{Li}^j be the inputs of capital and urban labor to the jth nonagricultural sector in period i.

Let Y_{Gi} be the outstanding stock of government infrastructure in period i.

The production of value added in sector j in period i is then given by the following:

$$va_{ji} = va_{ji}(y_{Ki}^j, y_{Li}^j, Y_{Gi})$$

We thus suppose that public infrastructure may act as a productivity increment to private production. Hence, production depends upon inputs of flows of capital and labor, while the productivity of those flow inputs depends upon the stock of public infrastructure. Thus, as an example, production uses the flow input of a truck. However, the efficiency of that truck is affected by the quality of the bridge, an item of publicly provided infrastructure. The intuition behind this specification is that public capital plays a role in the productivity of the real economy. Now, how does the private producer profit maximize over time?

13.6   Investment

In period i sector j pays income taxes on inputs of capital and labor given by t_{Kij}, t_{Lij}, respectively. There are no pure profits here since production functions are constant returns to scale, and hence the corporate income tax, which will be introduced shortly, is treated as a tax on returns to capital. We will treat investment as being sector specific, to be able to deal with different future rates of return, hence profit possibilities, across sectors. Each type of sectoral capital is produced via a sector-specific investment technology that uses inputs of capital and labor to produce new capital. Investment is carried out by the private sector and is entirely financed by domestic borrowing.

First, we will define the following notations and then use them in the model.

C_{Hi} = The cost of producing the quantity H of capital of a particular type in period i.

r_i = The interest rate in period i.

P_{Ki} = The return to capital in period i.

P_{Mi} = The price of money in period i.

δ_i = The rate of depreciation of capital.

In order to make an investment decision, the firm must estimate the expected intertemporal return on new capital. If C_{H1} is the cost-minimizing cost of producing the quantity of capital, H_1 in period 1, then the cost of borrowing must equal the present value of the return on new capital. Hence the following:

$$C_{H1} = \sum_{i=2}^{n} \left[\frac{P_{Ki}(1-\delta)^{i-2} H_1}{\prod_{j=1}^{i-1}(1+r_j)} \right] \tag{E13.2}$$

Here r_j is the interest rate in period j, given by the following:

$$r_j = 1/P_{Bj}$$

where P_{Bj} is the price of a bond in period j. Thus, the numerator of the RHS of eq. E13.2 represents the stream of nominal values of the depreciated newly created capital stock. The discount factor is the compounded intertemporal interest rates.

13.6.1   *Investment and tax evasion*

We now need to ask ourselves a basic question. Why does a firm pay the corporate income tax? One approach would be to say that the firm pays taxes to avoid the possible penalties that would be imposed if the firm is caught cheating.[3] The firm would also incorporate the probability of being caught. This approach would require us to somehow determine parameters that are exogenous to our model. Namely, what is the penalty for being caught evading taxes, and what is the probability of getting caught? Gordon and Li (2009) offer an approach to this topic.

13.7   Tax compliance

We will take a different approach to tax compliance. Essentially, we look at the after-tax return on investment in new capital. If the net return is positive, then the firm should pay taxes. If the net return is negative, then the firm will reduce its tax payments until it makes a positive after-tax profit. If the firm is not penalized for nonpayment, why should it pay any taxes at all? Here we will make another assumption. This assumption is that a firm that wishes to invest needs to finance that investment from the banking system. The banking system, on the other hand, requires a tax record from the firm in order to verify the firm's ability to pay. More formally, let us simplify by considering a two-period world. This will generate the necessary dynamics to illustrate our approach.

Suppose that

$$\frac{P_{K2}}{1+r_1} \geq t_{K1} \tag{E13.3}$$

This would mean that the present value of the return on new capital would be greater than the marginal capital tax rate (t_{K1}). In this case we assume the investor pays the full tax rate on capital inputs. Suppose, on the other hand, that

$$\frac{P_{K2}}{1+r_1} \leq t_{K1} \tag{E13.4}$$

Here the discounted rate of return is less than the tax rate. If the owner of the firm's capital were to pay the full statutory tax rate, then investment would be unprofitable, no investment would be undertaken, and the stock of capital would be static. We will suppose that in this case the investor reduces his tax payments so that he can break even on his investment.

We will thus suppose that the firm pays a modified tax rate of $\bar{t}_{K1}$ where

$$\bar{t}_{K1} = t_{K1} \left[1 - \left(\frac{t_{K1} - \dfrac{P_{K2}}{1+r_2}}{t_{K1}} \right)^{\alpha} \right] \tag{E13.5}$$

The term inside the brackets () represents the difference between the statutory tax rate and the present discounted value (PDV) of the return on new capital, that is, next period's rental rate discounted by next period's interest rate. This difference is then taken as a share of the statutory tax rate. This total is then subtracted from 1 to give a factor by which to modify the statutory tax rate. We obtain "actual" tax rate paid, t_{K1}. Here $0 \leq \alpha$ and higher values of α lead to lower values of taxes actually paid. That is, the ratio $\dfrac{\bar{t}_{K1}}{t_{K1}}$ reflects the share of the sector that operates in the underground economy. Hence α represents a firm-specific behavioral variable. An "honest" firm would set $\alpha = 0$, while a firm that is prone to evasion would have a high value for α.

This functional form for tax evasion is, admittedly, completely ad hoc. However, it does give us a form that can be calibrated (i.e., the value of α can be changed) so that the effective tax rate that is simulated approximates actual tax payments. Also, we will generate different effective rates for different sectors of the economy. These differences would reflect the different incentives for different sectors to evade their corporate income tax obligations.

13.8 Banking

In order to have forward-looking investors who borrow in order to finance investment, we need to also have forward-looking lenders. That is, we need to model a banking system in which banks consider the interest rate at which they lend, as well as the ability of the borrower to repay the loan. We will therefore describe a modeling approach that has certain similarities to the modeling approach we have to the intertemporal optimizing investor. Namely, our approach has ad hoc elements but permits calibration and behavioral analysis.

There is one bank for each aggregate sector of the economy. There are five such sectors, and hence five banks, corresponding to each of the aggregate capital stocks. Each bank lends primarily to the sector with which it is associated. Thus, for example, the agricultural development bank lends primarily to agriculture, the manufacturing bank to manufacturing, and so forth. Banks have no direct way of knowing whether specific firms operate in the underground economy or, more generally, the honesty of a firm. Banks only care about the amount of capital that they estimate the firm may have. If the firm defaults on its loan, then this represents the best estimate of the amount that the bank could seize from the borrowing firm. The bank will use the firm's tax returns as a tool to measure the firm's worth or propensity to default on debt.

The bank would, presumably, be willing to lend an amount equal or greater to its estimate of the firm's capital. The borrower is required to show the bank his tax returns in order to obtain a loan. The bank uses this tax return in the following way. Imagine that there is a single, flat corporate tax rate that the borrowing firm faces. Hence, suppose that T_{K1} represents taxes actually paid by the borrower in period 1. This is known to the bank as the potential borrower is required to present his tax returns. Thus, if the borrower fully complied with his tax obligation the value of his capital, $\hat{K}_1$, would be given by the following:

$$\hat{K}_1 = \frac{T_{K1}}{t_{K1}} \tag{E13.6}$$

In this case the bank lends an amount L_1, where $L_1 < C_{H1}$ and C_{H1} is the amount the investor would actually like to invest, as determined by (E13.2) earlier in this chapter. So how is this reduced amount determined?

Suppose that a simple functional form determines bank lending as a function of the amount requested as well as the estimated value of the firm's capital.

$$L_1 = C_{H1} \left[\frac{\dfrac{\hat{K}_1}{C_{H1}}}{1 + \dfrac{\hat{K}_1}{C_{H1}}} \right]^{\gamma} = C_{H1} \left[\frac{\hat{K}_1}{C_{H1} + \hat{K}_1} \right] \tag{E13.7}$$

Here γ represents a measure of risk aversion by the bank. If $\gamma = 0$, there are no credit restrictions, and the bank ignores estimates of the borrower's estimated net worth. As γ rises, the bank increasingly restricts lending if the term in brackets is less than one.

Notes

1 This type of formulation was introduced by Cagan (1956).
2 See Feltenstein and Shamloo (2013) for a discussion of this modeling approach.
3 This is the approach of Allingham and Sandmo (1972).

14 Financial assets in the dynamic CGE model (continued)

14.1 Why do we need financial assets? Theoretical purity versus the real world

In this chapter we will delve a bit deeper into the role of financial assets in a CGE model. Let us turn to the real world for intuition. In the previous chapter we talked about how we need a time dimension to realistically model savings behavior. Consumers must have expectations about the future, and these expectations are formed endogenously. The consumers can save by forgoing current consumption and purchasing financial assets that are costless to produce and which yield an endogenous rate of return. These financial assets are bonds, and we are essentially just replicating the macro identity:

$$S = I$$

14.2 Private investment and the sale of bonds

As the previous chapter discussed, private sector bonds are issued by investors who need to finance their current creation of capital by borrowing against anticipated future earnings on that capital. The government also produces bonds as a financing mechanism, but in this case as a different form of financing. Specifically, the government runs budget deficits and surpluses and, in the case of deficits, needs to borrow to pay its creditors. Let us now introduce a framework for the government that will be integrated into our CGE framework.

14.3 Financing the government budget deficit with the sale of public bonds

The government collects personal income, corporate profit, value-added taxes and sales taxes, as well as import duties. We may have many different tax rates in each category, so for example, different tax rates for different types of consumption goods. Similarly, we could have income tax rates differentiated by income level or type of labor.

What else does the government do? It pays to produce public goods, as well as for subsidies. Public goods are roads, bridges, parks, defense, health, education, and many other things. Subsidies are, for example, price supports designed

DOI: 10.4324/9780429295485-14

to shield consumers from rising costs of certain products. Another type of subsidy would be payments made to domestic manufacturers by government to allow these manufacturers to be more competitive on world markets. In fact, governments spend large shares of their overall budgets on such subsidies.

Finally, the government must cover both domestic and foreign interest obligations on public debt. As we shall see, the interest rate, $r = 1 / P_B$ where P_B is the price of bonds. Of course, this is standard macroeconomics, and we shall calculate P_B as part of the general equilibrium solution to our model. Hence, we will develop a model with standard macro characteristics. For example, as the government continues to run budget deficits, it needs to borrow more, hence supplying more bonds and raising the interest rate. Thus, its debt obligations rise, leading to yet higher interest rates.

In period 1 the deficit is given by the following:

$$D_1 = G_1 + S_1 + r_1 B_0 + r_{F1} e_1 B_{F0} - T_1 \qquad (E14.1)$$

Where
G_1 = spending on goods and services.
S_1 = subsidies.
$r_1 B_0$ = domestic interest obligations based on initial debt B_0.
$r_{F1} e_1 B_{F0}$ = foreign interest obligations, where r_{F1} is the foreign interest rate, e_1 is the exchange rate, and B_{F0} is the initial stock of foreign debt.
T_1 = tax revenues.

Public debt is the accumulation of annual deficits carried over from period to period. Thus, in period 2 the deficit is given by the following:

$$D_2 = G_2 + S_2 + r_2 \left(\Delta y_{BG1} + B_0 \right) + r_{F2} e_2 \left(C_{F1} + B_{F0} \right) - T_2 \qquad (E14.2)$$

The term $G_2 + S_2$ represents government spending on goods and services, plus subsidies in period 2. The term $r_2 \left(\Delta y_{BG1} + B_0 \right)$ is initial public debt, plus period 1 borrowing times the period 2 interest rate. The next expression, $r_{F2} e_2 \left(C_{F1} + B_{F0} \right)$, is the initial stock of foreign borrowing plus exogenous foreign borrowing in period 1, C_{F1}, all valued at the period 2 foreign interest rate and exchange rate. Finally, T_2 denotes tax collections in period 2.

The resulting deficit is financed by a combination of monetary expansion, as well as domestic and foreign borrowing. Accordingly, we have the following:

$$D_i = P_{Bi} \, \Delta y_{BGi} + P_{Mi} \Delta y_{Mi} + e_i C_{Fi} \qquad (E14.3)$$

The first term of (E14.3), $P_{Bi} \Delta y_{BGi}$, is domestic borrowing, that is, issuance of bonds. The second term, $P_{Mi} \Delta y_{Mi}$, is issuance of money. While the third term, $e_i C_{Fi}$, is foreign borrowing. We should note several things here. The introduction of money is not necessary for our dynamic model. Indeed, we do need a financial asset, "bonds," as a way to essentially borrow in one period and to repay in the next period.

However, recall that our goal is to replicate the real world and to be able to calibrate our model to real-world macroeconomics data.

There are several caveats to our approach. Perhaps the key one is the assumption that public and private debt are perfect substitutes. Our model does not have risk, and the solution is based upon short-term perfect foresight. Hence, the only way to differentiate between public and private debt would be to introduce an exogenous elasticity of substitution between the two. However, such a fixed, exogenous elasticity would be completely arbitrary and not impacted by demand or supply behavior. Another issue is that we assume that the only way for consumers to save is by buying bonds. They cannot save by purchasing durable goods. Effectively, when they buy private bonds, they are investing in the private capital that is financed by those bonds. They do not, however, own the new capital. Hence there is no savings by purchasing art, buildings, and so forth. We could introduce savings by having private demand for land. This would also introduce exogenous demand elasticities that are difficult to estimate and not necessary to the functioning of our model. Hence land enters as an input to production and the price of land is determined by how necessary it is for production.

14.4   The foreign sector

We now turn to the foreign sector and how it fits into this macro framework. We have already discussed a real model of trade between countries; however, we have not introduced the monetary approach to the balance of payments (BOP) and the consequences of having trade imbalances between countries. Indeed, in a model without financial assets, trade would be required to be equal in value across countries in much the same way as governments would be required to have balanced budgets. Otherwise, there is no financing mechanism. So let us now turn to a specification of the foreign sector with money. In order to determine the foreign demand for exports from the home country, we specify a simple equation that can be estimated with real data. Here exports from the home country depend upon relative price changes and change in the income of the rest of the world. So let us define the following variables:

ΔX_{wi} represents the percentage change in exports to the rest of the world in period i.

π_i represents the domestic rate of inflation in period i.

e_i is the exchange rate in period i.

π_{Fi} is the foreign rate of inflation.

y_{wi} is the world income in period i.

$$\Delta X_{wi} = \sigma_1 \left[\frac{\pi_1}{\Delta e_i + \pi_{Fi}} \right] + \sigma_2 \Delta y_{wi} \qquad (E14.4)$$

Δe_i is the percentage change in the exchange rate.

Δy_{wi} represents the percentage change in world income.

σ_1, σ_2 are elasticities. σ_1 is with respect to changes in the relative price levels at home and in the rest of the world (ROW). Presumably it is negative since if the home country's prices rise relative to the rest of the world, then the ROW's demand for the home country's exports should decline. Also σ_2 should be positive since a rise in world income should lead to an increase in demand for the home country's exports.

Trade and foreign borrowing will affect the domestic supply of money via the balance of payments. More specifically, the supply of foreign reserves available to the government in period i is given by the following:

$$y_{FGi} = y_{FG(i-1)} + X_i - IM_i + x_{F(i-1)} - x_{Fi} + C_{Fi} \qquad (E14.5)$$

Here x_{Fi} represents the demand for foreign monetary assets by citizens of the home country.

The term C_{Fi} represents exogenous foreign borrowing.

$X_i - IM_i$ is the current account balance, exports minus imports.

$x_{F(i-1)} - x_{Fi}$ represents private capital flows. In the context of our model, this is demand by consumers for foreign monetary assets.

The term y_{FGi} will thus be the total stock of foreign reserves (foreign money) in period i.

We thus have determined total changes in the monetary base caused by the foreign sector, from surpluses and deficits in the trade balance as well as changes in consumer demand for foreign assets (foreign currency). We can now do some simple accounting to arrive at the aggregate money.

Changes in the money supply are given by the following:

$$\Delta M_{Si} = \Delta y_{Mi} + \Delta OMO_i + e_i y_{FGi} - e_{i-1} y_{FG(i-1)} \qquad (E14.6)$$

Here Δy_{Mi} is determined from financing the budget deficit. If we have a truly independent central bank, then there can be no direct monetary financing of the deficit. In this case all direct financing would come via the Treasury's sale of bonds. However, in some countries the government can require the central bank to directly print money to cover the deficit. Normally, the central bank would create money, in our context, via open market operations. So let us make the following definitions:

ΔOMO_i is money created via open market operations.

$e_i y_{FGi} - e_{i-1} y_{FG(i-1)}$ is the domestic currency value of the BOP.

We have now determined money supply changes essentially from the demand side. That is, we are treating banks as passive actors. However, a more realistic approach would be to introduce banks as active participants in the monetary process. Intuitively, the bank is a profit-making entity that makes loans to investors who wish to finance investments in forward-looking projects. We will, for now, ignore private borrowing used to finance consumption. In other words, no mortgages, car loans, or other such personal loans are considered. Further, the borrower is a corporation, which approaches the bank with a project proposal that has a certain anticipated rate of return on investment. The corporation has risk associated with it. Namely, the firm may default on its loan payments. This default would occur if the firm's return on its investment falls below the value of its debt. Essentially, the future does not work out as expected. Mechanically, how would this happen, and what would banks do so as to anticipate the possibility?

14.5 Banking, defaults, and credit constraints

Recall from Chapter 13 that investment is given by the following:

$$C_{H1} = \sum_{i=2}^{n} \left[\frac{P_{Ki}(1-\delta)^{i-2} H_1}{\prod_{j=1}^{i-1}(1+r_j)} \right] \tag{E13.2}$$

Hence the value of the cost of construction (amount borrowed) is C_{H1} to produce the quantity of capital H_1 is equal to the present discounted value (PDF) of the nominal stream of earning from H_1, discounted the by the nominal interest rates in each period.

If at some point the present value of investment, as given previously, falls below the corresponding value of debt service, then the sector is unable to pay its debt obligations, which were incurred to finance this investment. This situation might occur if, after the investment was incurred, the interest rate rose or the rate of return to capital fell due to some unanticipated event. We assume that a bankrupt firm cannot invest. Thus, at this point the firm is insolvent and stops making payments on its existing obligations. The bank which holds these assets now holds corresponding bad debts.

Because of the uncertainty of the future, both the borrower and the bank might change their behavior based upon their perception of the likelihood of a default on the loan. We will suppose that the compensating behavior is entirely carried out by the bank. Effectively this amounts to saying that investor will not be subject to penalties if he defaults. Who else suffers if the investor defaults? The answer, of course, is the bank that loses the entire value of the loan it made to the investor. Accordingly, the bank wishes to guard against such failures by restricting its loans according to some mechanical strategy.

Suppose that banks follow a strategy of lending that looks at the risks associated with their borrowers. As their borrowers become more insolvent, the banks ration credit to those borrowers. It should be noted that we do not have a specific measure of risk. Rather, we are substituting accumulated bad debt as a proxy for risk. We will choose a simple functional form that connects credit rationing to borrower insolvency.

Suppose, as before, that C_{Hij} is the demand for borrowing by sector j in period i. Suppose also that bank k has Def_{ik} percent of its total assets in default in period i. Let $\delta_{ik} > 0$ be a parameter specific to bank k, and let β_{jk} be the share of borrowing by sector j taken by bank k. Sector j then receives loans L_{ji}, where

$$L_{ji} = \sum \beta_{jk} \left(1 - \delta_k Def_{ik}\right) C_{Hij} \tag{E14.7}$$

Thus, if there are no bank assets in default, then no credit rationing takes place. If assets are in default, then the credit demanded by sector j for investment is reduced by each bank proportionally to the share of that bank's defaulted assets in total assets.

In our applications of this model, we generally simplify things by assuming that there is one bank associated with each sector of the economy. This is a rough approximation of reality in many developing countries where, for example, there is a single agricultural development bank, a single manufacturing bank, yet another one for tourism, etc. In this case we would have

$$\beta_{jk} = 1.0 \; for \, 1 \, value \, of \, k$$

We could also reflect differences in bank attitude to default risk by allowing for different values of δ_{ik} for different banks. For example, a value of $\delta_{ik} = 0$ would mean that bank k does not care if its borrowers have bad debts. It always lends the full value of the loan request. As δ_{ik} rises, the bank reduces its actual loan, relative to the amount requested.

We have now specified the supply side of the monetary economy. That is, we have functional forms that connect the central bank's supply of money to various exogenous and endogenous variables. In particular, the exogenous variable δ_{ik} reflects a degree of risk aversion by the bank. If, for example, δ_{ik} is high, then the bank greatly reduces its loan relative to the firm's request if the firm already has assets in default. If, on the other hand, $\delta_{ik} = 0$, then no matter how bad the firm's defaulted debts are, the bank still lends the full amount of the request, C_{Hij}.

Now we need to formulate the demand for financial assets. As we have discussed earlier, corporations demand assets in order to finance investment. Consumers demand financial assets in order to save for future consumption. Intuitively, we have a world in which the only durable assets are factors, land, and labor, and no intermediate goods are durable. Also, the consumer may wish to anticipate a future in which, for example, he stops working so that the value of his initial endorsement of labor goes to zero. In this case, he would need to hold financial assets in order to finance his retirement.

So let us now consider the formulation of the problem of a consumer who consumes and saves for the future. He has perfect foresight for two periods and then a set of future expectations that are based on a weighted average of past outcomes. He then chooses in each discrete time period an optimal pattern of savings and consumption so as to optimize his intertemporal utility. Let us now turn to the consumer's specification.

Consumption

$$\text{Max } U(x), \; x = \left(x_1, x_{Lu1}, x_{Lr1}, x_2, x_{Lu2}, x_{Lr2}\right) \tag{E14.8a}$$

such that

$$\left(1 + t_i\right) P_i x_i + P_{Lui} x_{Lui} + p_{Lri} x_{Lri} + P_{Mi} x_{Mi} + P_{Bi} x_{Bi} + e_i P_{Bfi} x_{Bfi} = C_i \tag{E14.8b}$$

$$\log(L_{ui} / L_{ri}) = a_1 + a_2 \log \frac{P_{Lui} - P_{Lri}}{P_{Lui} + P_{Lri}} \tag{E14.8c}$$

$$\log P_{Mi} x_{Mi} = a + b \, \log\left(1 + t_i\right) P_i x_i - c \log r_i, c = c\left(DEF / ASSETT\right) \tag{E14.8d}$$

$$P_{B2} x_{B2} = d_0 + d_1 \left(1 + t_2\right) P_2 x_2 + d_2 \left[\frac{r_2 - \pi_2}{1 + \pi_2}\right] \tag{E14.8e}$$

Where

P_i = price vector of consumption goods in period i.
x_i = vector of consumption in period i.
C_i = value of aggregate consumption in period i (including purchases of financial assets).
N_i = aggregate income in period i (including potential income from the sale of real and financial assets).
t_i = vector of value-added tax rates in period i.
P_{Lui} = price of urban labor in period i.
L_{ui} = allocation of total labor to urban labor in period i.
x_{Lui} = demand for urban leisure in period i.
P_{Lri} = price of rural labor in period i.
L_{ri} = allocation of total labor to rural labor in period i.
x_{Lri} = demand for rural leisure in period i.
a_2 = elasticity of rural/urban migration.
P_{Ki} = price of capital in period i.
K_0 = initial holding of capital.
P_{Ai} = price of land in period i.
A_0 = initial holding of land.
δ = rate of depreciation of capital.
P_{Mi} = price of money in period i. Money in period 1 is the numeraire and hence has a price of 1.
x_{Mi} = holdings of money in period i.
P_{Bi} = discount price of a certificate of deposit in period i.
π_i = domestic rate of inflation in period i.

r_i, r_{Fi} = the domestic and foreign interest rates in period i.

x_{Bi} = quantity of bank deposits, that is, CD's in period i.

e_i = the exchange rate in terms of units of domestic currency per unit of foreign currency in period i.

x_{BFi} = quantity of foreign currency held in period i.

TR_i = transfer payments from the government in period i.

a, b, α, β = estimated constants.

d_i = constants estimated from model simulations.

For simplicity of exposition, we will limit ourselves to a two-period time horizon here, the same methodology works for longer periods. Equation (E14.8a) represents the utility of the consumer. He maximizes overconsumption of goods and leisure, both urban and rural. Equation (E14.8b) is the value of his consumption of goods and leisure, plus expenditures on financial assets.

Equation (E14.8c) is a migration equation that explains changes in the relative holdings of urban and rural labor by using changes in relative urban rural wages. Finally, equations (E14.d) and (E14.4e) are, respectively, demand for money and demand for bonds behavioral equations in which demand for the financial assets depend upon income, interest rates, and level of defaulted assets. The parameters in these equations are all to be estimated from past data.

We are now in a position to solve the intertemporal model with endogenous interest rates, rates of inflation, and growth. We can also incorporate endogenous personal behavioral variables, such as savings rates and migration rates. Thus, our model can be very different from the CGE models that impose exogenous savings rates and thus generate essentially exogenous growth rates.

15 Monetization and the introduction of a central bank

15.1 Why do consumers hold money? A simple cash-in-advance specification

We have introduced most of the basic elements in a macroeconomic model. We have specified a simple discrete time structure for the dynamics of the model. Consumers have short-term perfect foresight with adaptive expectations for the longer term. In this framework we have introduced consumer savings as the outcome of optimizing behavior in which the individual distributes consumption over time to maximize utility. The consumer does so by purchasing interest-bearing bonds, which are issued by private sector investors, who sell them in order to finance investments. There are also public bonds issued by the government which uses the bonds to finance budget deficits. Public and private bonds are risk-free and, therefore, are essentially the same product.

Hence, we have, so far, created a model with time, production, consumption, savings, and investment. There is also a single financial asset, bonds. What is missing? The answer is money, which is used as a medium of exchange. It is difficult to introduce money in an axiomatic manner into our model. There is a long macro literature that attempts to do so, but we will not attempt to incorporate these approaches here. Rather, we will use a simple cash-in-advance model. This model has a long history and is quite simple to implement. The underlying intuition of this approach is that agents need cash to carry out transactions. Accordingly, if one plans on current and future consumption, then one must hold cash balances in advance of making those current consumption purchases. The real-world analogy would be that people need to hold checking account balances before they go to the store to buy things. We thus need to expand upon the model of the consumer, who now requires money. We will also introduce a central bank that creates money via open market operations.

For presentational purposes, we will assume that there is a single consumer in our model who has perfect foresight in all markets. He maximizes an intertemporal utility function subject to his expectation of future price changes, which are incorporated into his budget constraint. Let $x_i = (x_{1i}, \ldots x_{Ni})$ be the consumer's consumption vector in period i and let x_{Li} be his consumption of leisure. We will assume that the consumer receives utility only from two activities: the consumption of goods generated by the input-output matrix and leisure. He is required to

DOI: 10.4324/9780429295485-15

cover his expenditures from income in each period, and he pays ad valorem tax rates $\{t\} = \{t_{1i}, \ldots t_{Ni}\}$ on the consumption of goods in period i. In order to derive a simple analytical expression, we will also assume that he receives utility only from consumption in the first T time periods, although we will impose a savings rate in the final period. The consumer's utility function is of the following form:

$$\prod_{i=1}^{T} x_{L_i}^{\alpha_i} \left\{ \prod_{j=1}^{n} x_{ji}^{\alpha_{ji}} \right\} \tag{E15.1}$$

In practice we will assume that exponential discounting is used so that $\alpha_{j(i+1)} = \alpha_{ji} / (1+\sigma)$ where $\sigma \geq 0$ is the rate of time preference. Hence, equation (E15.1) may be written in log-linear form as follows:

$$\sum_{i=1}^{T} 1/(1+\sigma)^{i-1} \left\{ \alpha_i \log x_{Li} + \sum_{j=1}^{N} \alpha_{j1} \log x_{ji} \right\} \tag{E15.2}$$

The consumer's problem is thus to maximize his utility function subject to

$$(1+t_j)P_j x_j + P_{Lj} x_{Lj} + P_{Mj} x_{Mj} + P_{Mj} x_{Bj} + e_j x_{BFj} \leq \bar{Y}_j \tag{E15.3}$$

Where the right-hand side of the equation represents the budget constraint, which in period j is given by

$$\bar{Y}_j = (1-\sigma)^j P_{Kj} K_0 + P_{Lj} L_0 + TR_j \tag{E15.4}$$

and

$$(1+t_j)P_j x_j + P_{Lj} x_{Lj} + P_{Mj} x_{Mj} + P_{Mj} x_{Bj} + e_j x_{BFj} \leq \bar{Y}_j + P_{M(j-1)} x_{M(j-1)}$$
$$+ P_{Mj} x_{Bj} + e_j (1+r_{Fj}) x_{BF} \tag{E15.5}$$

This is simply an intertemporal budget constraint. We define x_{Mi}, x_{Bi}, and x_{BFi} as the consumer's demand for money, domestic, and foreign bonds, respectively, in period i, and e_i, as the exchange rate in period i. Here e_i is defined as the domestic currency price of foreign assets. In addition, r_{Fi} is the exogenously given foreign interest rate. Finally, TR_i represents any transfer payments the consumer receives from the government, while K_0, L_0, M_0, B_0, and B_{F0} are his initial allocations of capital, labor, money, domestic, and foreign bonds, respectively.

The consumer is assumed to face two additional constraints. The first of these is a cash constraint that connects his holdings of money to his consumption and the interest rate. Accordingly, we set the following:

$$P_{Mj} x_{Mj} / \left[(1+t_j)P_j x_j \right] = ar_j^{-b} \tag{E15.6}$$

Hence, there is an obvious trade-off between current consumption and money holdings. Since money is carried over from period to period, as in the utility implications of changes in the interest rate are not necessarily clear. We thus use a modified cash-in-advance formulation of money demand in which money demand depends not only upon the value of consumption but also upon the interest rate, reflecting opportunity cost. This is thus an imposed condition reflecting, we assume, institutional constraints rather than an outcome derived from optimizing behavior.

To be completely consistent with the structure of a perfect foresight general equilibrium model, consumers should choose between domestic and foreign assets on the basis of future returns; the consumer should only hold the asset with the higher total yield since there is no risk. We wish, however, to permit simultaneous holdings of both domestic and foreign assets. We therefore impose a constraint that has the same ad hoc characteristic as the constraint on money demand. The second additional constraint is that we assume that domestic and foreign bonds are not perfect substitutes and that the consumer chooses between them according to relative domestic and foreign total bond yields, deflated by the anticipated exchange rate change.[1] Thus, exchange rate changes along with relative domestic and foreign interest rates to determine consumer savings and hence have direct welfare effects.

Finally, we close the consumer's problem by assuming that his savings rate in period T is given by an exogenous constant. The consumer does not receive utility from this savings. If savings are given by holdings of domestic plus foreign assets, then[2]

$$P_{BT}x_{BT} + e_T x_{BFT} = s\left(1 + t_T\right)P_T x_T \tag{E15.7}$$

Equation (E14.7) is an ad hoc closure rule which, as the closure period T becomes greater, becomes less significant in early time periods.

Our use of money constraint, although apparently ad hoc, could be replaced by an equivalent formulation that incorporates money into the utility function. Our current formulation, however, permits direct estimation, which will be important later. We notice that since domestic bonds are short term, $P_{B,i+1}x_{Bi}$ reflects both principal and interest in period $i + 1$ on a bond purchased in period i. See Feltenstein and Morris (1990) for the solution to this consumer maximization problem.

15.2   Budget deficits and the adjustment of the exchange rate

Here, we continue the discussion on public deficit covered in Chapter 14 and add the concept of exchange rate to that model. Thus, let T_i be the total taxes collected by the government in period i and let G_i be the value of its expenditures on goods and services in the same period.[3] If $Y_{BG(i-1)}$ is the government's issue of bonds in period $i-1$, then its budget deficit, D_i, in period i is

$$D_i = G_i + P_{Mi}y_{BG(i-1)} + e_i r_{Fi} \sum_{j=1}^{i-1}\left(D_{F0} + C_{Fi} - AM_i\right) - T_i \tag{E15.8}$$

where C_{Fi} is the gross foreign borrowing of the government in period i, AM_i is its amortization C_{Fi} of foreign debt, and D_{F0} is its initial foreign debt. Accordingly, the term in parentheses is the outstanding foreign debt of the government.

The government finances this deficit, if D_i is positive, from three sources: sales of bonds, government issuance of money, and foreign borrowing. We will assume that the government's gross foreign borrowing in period i, C_{Fi}, is exogenously determined. Accordingly, the domestically financed portion of the budget deficit is given by $D_i - C_{Fi}$. Let s_{Bi} be that portion of the domestic financing requirements in period i that is covered by the sale of domestic bonds. Here s_{Bi} is any continuous function of P_{Bi}, the price of bonds. Thus, the government's issue of money and bonds in period i,[4] y_{Mi} and y_{Bi}, is given by E15.9 and E15.10, respectively.

$$P_{Mi} y_{Mi} = (1 - s_{Bi})(D_i - C_{Fi}) \qquad \text{(E15.9)}$$

$$P_{Bi} y_{Bi} = s_{Bi}(D_i - C_{Fi}) \qquad \text{(E15.10)}$$

If, on the other hand, D_i is negative, that is, a surplus, then D_i is paid out as transfer payments to the consumer, TR_i.

Apart from producing infrastructure, collecting taxes, and financing the budget deficit, the government also determines an exchange rate regime. There are many possible such regimes. For example, we could have a fixed exchange rate regime in which the home currency is pegged to a major international currency, usually the US\$. An alternative system might have the government changing the exchange rate as its demand for foreign reserves changes. This sort of "leaning against the wind" system is used in Feltenstein and Morris (1990). Yet another alternative would be a floating exchange rate system in which the government (central bank) leaves the exchange rate to be determined by the free market. Let us give a brief description of the "leaning against the wind" approach since it is typical of many developing countries. The supply of foreign reserves, Y_{FGi}, available to the government in period i is given by

$$Y_{FGi} = Y_{FG(i-1)} + X_i - IM_i + x_{F(i-1)} - x_{Fi} + C_{Fi} \qquad \text{(E14.5)}$$

Here x_{Fi} represents the demand for foreign assets by citizens of the home country, so $x_{F(i-1)} - x_{Fi}$ represents private capital flows, while X_i and IM_i are exports and imports, respectively. All terms on the right-hand side of equation (E14.5) are solved from the maximization problems of the domestic and foreign consumer. What is the demand of the government for foreign assets?

Consider Figure 15.1, which represents the government's exchange rate policy in period i. The horizontal axis represents the market exchange rate in period i, e_i *(e.g., dollars per 1 Euro)*, while the vertical axis represents the government's demand for foreign assets. In addition, let x_{Fi} represent the government's critical level of foreign reserves in period i. This critical level is determined exogenously and is not necessarily related to the current inflow of foreign currency. For example, a typical guidance from the International Monetary Fund in the past was to take this critical level to be equal to three months of imports.

15.3   The other source of money creation: capital flows in the open economy model

Let us assume that a particular exchange rate in period i, e_i as shown in Figure 15.1, is depreciated from the previous period. Hence, $e_i > e_{i-1}$.[5] In this case we can determine a well-defined government demand for reserves, x_{FGi} in Figure 15.1 and given formally by E15.11:

$$x_{FGi} = f_i(e_i) \qquad\qquad (E15.11)$$

where f_i is any continuous, monotonically decreasing function. Equivalently, if there is a slight decrease in the equilibrium supply of, and hence demand for, foreign reserves by the government below its critical level, then there is a sharp depreciation in the exchange rate. The critical level corresponds with (e_{i-1}, x_{Fi}). We may then construct excess demand by the government for foreign reserves, D_{Fi}, as follows:

$$D_{Fi} = x_{FGi} - y_{FGi} \qquad\qquad (E15.12)$$

Where y_{FGi} is the supply of foreign exchange available to the government in period i. In particular, we see that if $e_i > e_{i-1}$, then large increases in the exchange rate, e, cause only a small decrease in x_{FGi} since the demand is relatively flat. If, in equation (E14.5), the current account improves more rapidly than the capital account deteriorates in response to the depreciation, then there will be a net decrease in D_{Fi} in equation (E15.12). Thus, increases in e_i above e_{i-1} tend to increase the supply of foreign assets for the government, thereby driving e_i down towards e_{i-1}. Suppose on the other hand that $e_i < e_{i-1}$. In this region small changes in e_i cause large shifts in x_{FGi}. Thus, in a particular situation, a decrease in e_i, an appreciation, will cause a sharp increase in government demand for reserves, x_{FGi}, leading to an increase in excess demand by the government for foreign reserves, D_{Fi}. Hence, the foreign currency price of dollars increases, and the exchange rate tends to move back towards e_{i-1}.

Thus, the government creates a correspondence between changes in the exchange rate and movements away from the critical level of reserves. If, as an extreme case, the graph in Figure 15.1 becomes horizontal at x_{Fi}, then this corresponds to a pure float when reserves fall to their critical level. This is the scenario of much of the balance of payments crisis literature, which thus may be viewed as a special case of our model. A graph that is close to horizontal below x_{Fi} may be taken as representing the policy of a nervous government, while a graph that is closer to vertical reflects a relatively unconcerned policy.

The demonstration of an existence of equilibrium is straightforward. The only problem arises from the fact that the government's issuance of bonds or money in each period increases as the corresponding prices drop, thus leading

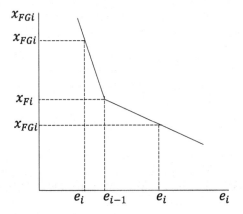

Figure 15.1 Exchange rate and government demand for reserves

to a downward-sloping supply curve. For example, as the price of domestic bonds falls, the government must increase its bond sales in order to finance a particular budget deficit. We can circumvent this problem and prove the existence of an equilibrium in a relatively straightforward way (see Feltenstein and Morris 1990).

15.4   The CGE model now becomes a recognizable macro model

Let us summarize the model extensions we have introduced. We now have a structure that has time dimensions, in terms of discrete time periods. We have consumers who have forward-looking expectations. These consumers optimize by allocating consumption over time and do so by saving. Their saving is created by the purchase of bonds, which are created by both the government, to finance budget deficits, as well as by the privated sector, to finance investment. In addition, consumers have a cash-in-advance demand for money, which is needed for transactions. Thus consumption and production, via investment, are dynamic and forward looking. We also have a foreign sector that exports to and imports from the home country and, hence, generates a balance of payments. There is a foreign currency and either a fixed or floating exchange rate regime.

We are thus in a position to generate results that are familiar to a macroeconomist. Our model will have rates of real GDP growth, as well as inflation rates. In addition we will generate endogenous budget deficits and financing instruments for those deficits. We will also have trade deficits (or surpluses) and capital flows. At the same time, we will have micro information that is not available in a traditional macro model. For example, we will have disaggregated outputs giving consumption for any number of consumers. We will also have sectoral outputs for as many sectors as there are in the input-output matrix.

Notes

1 As before, see Feltenstein and Morris (1990) for the specific functional form of this asset substitution.
2 This savings rate closure rule is equivalent to an exogenous bequest rule. An example of such a bequest rule is given in Fair (1984, ch. 3).
3 We have a small inconsistency in notation here. We are using T to denote both total tax revenue, as well as the final time period. Also, we use $L_1 \Rightarrow C_{H1}$ to denote a sectoral tax rate.
4 This is done through open market operations.
5 This simply means that the current endogenous supply of foreign reserves differs from the given supply of reserves from the previous period.

16 CGE models and their application to developing countries

The example of tax evasion and the underground economy

CGE analysis has been applied to many developing countries in order to study policy changes that are, in a sense, "out of sample." By this we mean that they have never been tried before, or that there is insufficient data to use econometric techniques to project what the outcomes of these policies might be. In this chapter, we would like to introduce a topic that is very important in developing countries. This topic is tax evasion and, more particularly, the presence of an underground economy. That is, a sector of the overall economy that is often very large and which avoids government taxation and regulation. Because of this large, tax-evading sector, CGE models that impose statutory tax rates often overpredict tax revenues when applied to developing countries. The issue of tax evasion in developing countries is addressed in Johnson et al. (1997).

In a recent paper,[1] we develop a dynamic CGE model, applied to Pakistan, in which optimizing agents evade taxes by operating in the underground economy. The cost to firms of evading taxes is that they find themselves subject to credit rationing from banks. Our model simulations show that in the absence of budgetary flexibility to adjust expenditures, which is typical of developing countries, raising tax rates too high drives firms into the underground economy, thereby reducing the tax base. Aggregate investment in the economy is lowered because of credit rationing. Taxes that are too low eliminate the underground economy but result in unsustainable budget and trade deficits. Thus, the optimal rate of taxation, from a macroeconomic point of view, may lead to some underground activity.

16.1 Background

In many developing and transition countries, economic activity in the unreported sector is more than 40 percent of GDP.[2] Heavy tax burden and excessive regulation imposed by governments that lack the capability to enforce compliance are widely regarded as driving firms into the underground economy. This diversion into unofficial activity undermines the tax base and can significantly affect public finances and the quality of public administration. The illegal nature of underground activity also constrains private investment and growth. For instance, firms operating underground are often unable to make use of market-supporting institutions like the

DOI: 10.4324/9780429295485-16

judicial system and courts and, as a result, may underinvest. One important cost imposed by the inability to enforce legal contracts is the limited access to formal credit markets.

Here we will develop a simple intertemporal general equilibrium model with heterogeneous agents and credit rationing to explain the prevalence of large underground economies in many developing and transition countries.[3] We explore the link between tax rates, access to credit, and the size of the undisclosed sector and examine the consequences of the underground economy for public finances and aggregate economic performance. Entry and exit into the underground economy are derived as part of optimizing behavior that depends on taxes and interest rates. Firms operating underground are subject to credit rationing by banks, which reduce loans in relation to the firm's nonpayment of taxes. This assumption is consistent with the observation, e.g., Johnson et al. (1997), that it may be more difficult for tax evaders to borrow from a bank because to do so would require official documentation, especially if the bank requires collateral and if the process of hiding economic activity involves concealing the true ownership of assets.[4]

Since the size of the underground economy in the paper depends upon both endogenous and exogenous variables, our framework has scope for policy changes. The endogenous variables lend themselves to analysis via a CGE approach. We address the issue of policy responses towards the emergence of underground activity and emphasize the ambiguous effects of taxation by means of numerical simulations for Pakistan. This should be viewed as an illustrative example of a developing country which faces problems from tax evasion and parallel markets for both goods and financial assets. Economic reform will depend upon policies that reduce the various forms of tax evasion, especially given the challenges typical of developing country with controlling its budget deficit. This analysis is thus an example of an issue, tax evasion, that is quite typical of developing countries and which lends itself to a CGE approach.

16.2 Tax evasion in developing countries

There have been a number of empirical studies of the scope of the underground economy in developing countries (see Schnieder and Enste (2000) for a survey). See Dervis et al. (1981, 1982) for a general study of developing countries in a general equilibrium context. Most of these studies use proxies, such as the amount of cash in circulation, or electricity consumption to estimate the size of the underground economy. In addition, they are not derived from optimizing models, but are based upon ad hoc empiricism. Accordingly, they can at best be used for partial equilibrium analysis and hence may lead to inaccurate conclusions. So how should we approach the issues of the underground economy and tax evasion?

High statutory tax rates and onerous official regulations are widely cited as explanations for why entrepreneurs go underground (See de Soto (1989), Johnson et al. (1997), among others). Following these empirically based studies, a number of theoretical papers have followed Allingham and Sandmo (1972). Here there are exogenously given probabilities of being caught for tax evasions, as well as exogenously given increased rates of corporate profitability caused by tax evasion. There are several problems with this approach. Most importantly, it depends upon exogenous, enforced penalties for getting caught evading taxes. Thus, there is no room for behavioral differences between agents. In addition, there is no role for a banking system. In practice, firms require a tax history in order to qualify for investment financing from the banking system. Hence firms that wish to invest may have an incentive to comply with their tax obligations.

Our paper also models the benefits from operating in terms of the firm's desire to evade corporate taxes. This assumption is consistent with the observation that in many developing countries, taxes on formal firms constitute a major source of government revenues, and narrow tax bases for formal firms have often resulted in governments imposing very high marginal tax rates.[5]

The cost of operating in the underground economy is modeled in terms of the inability to borrow from the official banking system.[6] Banks in the model are assumed not to have perfect information about the firm's true ownership of assets and its associated true tax obligation. We assume that due to collateral requirements credit is provided only in relation to the firm's implied ownership of assets, which is determined from its actual tax payment. The idea here is that in the face of default, banks can only seize those assets that have been officially declared by the firm. Hence, the higher extent of tax evasion leads to the lower bank's implied value of firm assets and the lower amount of credit provided by the banking system. Our approach has some similarity to Kiyotaki and Moore (1997), who model credit limits on loans. These limits are determined by estimates of collateral which, in turn, are determined by the values of durable asset holdings by borrowers. Here, tax payments are used to estimate the value of the durable asset of the borrower as the asset cannot be directly observed.

We assume that firms can operate partially in the formal and partially in the underground economy. That part of their operation that takes place in the legal economy pays taxes and can borrow from the banking system. The part of operations that is underground does not pay taxes and cannot borrow. Admittedly this distinction is artificial but captures some of the benefits and costs of operating in the underground economy discussed in the literature. In reality, the underground firm may still be able to finance its investment needs by relying on trade credits or borrowing from secondary lenders who charge higher than market interest rates and are willing to incur high risks.[7] Presumably, in the absence of legal enforcement of contracts and inadequate or weak business networks and supplier relationships, this would further increase the costs of operating underground.

Our approach also assumes that firms can evade taxes without any real risk of detection or punishment. From a modeling perspective, it is difficult to determine just what the penalty for tax evasion should be. That is, should it be a criminal penalty or a fine? Should it be proportional to the size of the tax evasion, or should it be a flat rate? In addition, what is the probability of apprehension faced by a tax evader? Presumably this probability should itself be some function of the enforcement technology, the amount of evasion, as well as the amount of money spent on enforcement. A problem with that modeling strategy is that, as there is no clear mapping from the enforcement technology and how spending affects the probability of being caught to real data, it does not offer a reasonable framework for quantitative evaluations. Moreover, Shleifer and Vishny (1993) point out that relatively weak public pressure on corruption or the enforcement ability of the government – as we believe to be the case in many developing countries – represents in fact a fitting assumption on tax evasion.

In our model, the decision to operate in the underground economy depends on the firm's present value of the future stream of returns on marginal investment relative to the corporate capital tax rate. If the marginal rate of return is higher than the corporate tax rate, the firm chooses to operate in the formal economy since it is profitable to borrow and pay taxes. If, on the other hand, the tax rate is greater than the marginal rate of return on investment, the firm chooses to operate in the underground economy. However, we assume that the firm does not make a bipolar choice. That is, it reduces its tax payments and borrowing for investment proportionally to the difference between the rate of return and the tax rate. The firm may face four possible options, as outlined here. Hence (a) if the rate of return were zero, then the firm would pay no taxes and carry out no borrowing for investment; (b) if the rate of return on investment were lower than taxes, then the firm would pay only a portion of taxes; (c) if tax rates and rates of return on investment were equal, then the firm would pay the full tax rate and invest; (d) if the rate of return on investment was higher than tax rate, then the firm would pay the full taxes.

In this framework, one could measure the size of the underground economy by aggregating the value of all lost tax revenues and comparing it to the revenues that would accrue if rates were low enough so as to generate no underground activity. The ratio of the two would then provide a measure of the share of the underground economy in total economic activity. We would thus compare two simulated equilibria.

16.3   A general equilibrium specification

In this section we develop the formal structure of a dynamic general equilibrium model that endogenously generates an underground economy. Much of the structure of our model is designed to permit numerical implementation. Our model has n discrete time periods. All agents optimize in each period over a two-period time horizon. That is, in period t they optimize given prices for periods t and $t+1$ and expectations for prices for the future after $t+1$. When period $t+2$ arrives, agents reoptimize for period $t+2$ and $t+3$, based on new information about period $t+2$.

Our model structure is related to a number of earlier papers, starting with Strotz (1956). Here preferences are inconsistent over time, primarily because the future does not turn out as anticipated. Thus, it may be optimal for agents to commit themselves for a few periods into the future. They may be better off, however, if they reoptimize at some later date, based on their own changed preferences or changes in economic variables. This is quite different from the notion of time inconsistency of Kydland and Prescott (1977), where rational behavior by economic agents itself leads to inconsistencies in what would otherwise be an optimal government plan. Much of this chapter is taken from Feltenstein et al. (2017).

16.3.1   *Production*

Similar to Chapter 13, there are eight factors of production and three types of financial assets as shown in Table 16.1:

The five types of capital correspond to five aggregate nonagricultural productive sectors.[8] An input-output matrix, A_t, is used to determine intermediate and final production in period t. Corresponding to each sector in the input-output matrix, sector-specific value added is produced using capital and urban labor for the nonagricultural sectors, and land and rural labor in agriculture.

Assuming that there are more than five sectors in the economy, the different factors would be allocated across the economy so that agriculture uses land and rural labor, and all other sectors use one of the five capital types plus urban labor. Accordingly, capital is perfectly mobile across a given subsector but is immobile across other subsectors. Labor, on the other hand, may migrate from the rural to the urban sector.[9]

The specific formulation of the firm's problem is as follows. Let y_{Ki}^j, y_{Li}^j be the inputs of capital and urban labor to the jth nonagricultural sector in period i. Let Y_{Gi} be the outstanding stock of government infrastructure in period i. The production of value added in sector j in period i is then given by the following:

$$va_{ji} = va_{ji}(y_{Ki}^j, y_{Li}^j, Y_{Gi}) \qquad\qquad (E16.1)$$

Where we suppose that public infrastructure may act as a productivity increment to private production.

Sector j pays income taxes on inputs of capital and labor, given by t_{Kji}, t_{Lji} respectively, in period i. The interpretation of these taxes is that the capital tax, t_{Kji}, is a tax on firm profits, while the labor tax, t_{Lji}, is a personal income tax that is withheld at source.

We suppose that each type of sectoral capital is produced via a sector-specific investment technology that uses inputs of capital and labor to produce new capital. Investment is carried out by the private sector and is entirely financed by domestic borrowing.[10]

Table 16.1 Production

Factors of production:	*Financial assets:*
1–5. Capital types	9. Domestic currency
6. Urban labor	10. Bank deposits
7. Rural labor	11. Foreign currency
8. Land	

Let us define the following notation:

C_{Hi} = cost of producing the quantity H of capital of a particular type in period i.
r_i = interest rate in period i.
P_{Ki} = return to capital in period i.
P_{Mi} = price of money in period i.
δ_i = The rate of depreciation of capital.

Suppose, then, that the rental price of capital in period 1 is P_1. If C_{H1} is the cost-minimizing cost of producing the quantity of capital, H_1, then the cost of borrowing must equal the present value of the return on new capital. Hence

$$C_{H1} = \sum_{i=2}^{n} \left[\frac{P_{Ki}(1-\delta)^{i-2} H_1}{\prod_{j=1}^{i-1}(1+r_j)} \right] \qquad \text{(E16.2)}$$

Where the interest rate in period j is given by the following:

$$r_j = 1/P_{Bj} \qquad \text{(E16.3)}$$

Here P_{Bj} is the price of a bond in period j. The tax on capital is implicitly included in the investment problem, as capital taxes are paid on capital as an input to production.

The decision to invest depends not only on the variables in the previous equation but also upon the decision the firm makes as to whether it should pay taxes.[11] This decision determines the firm's entry into the underground economy. We assume that the firm's decision is based upon a comparison of the tax rate on capital with the rate of return on new capital. As discussed earlier in the chapter, if the tax rate on capital is less than or equal to the corresponding rate of return, the firm pays the full tax. There are two options when a firm chooses to operate in the underground economy, which include the situation when the tax rate is greater than the return to new capital and the firm pays less than the full capital tax or if the firm's return on investment is zero and the firms evades the full tax liability. Therefore, due to the last two options, the firm withdraws, at least partially, into the underground economy.[12] Formally, suppose that we were in a two-period world. Suppose that

$$\frac{P_{K2}}{1+r_1} \geq t_{K1} \qquad \text{(E16.4)}$$

That is, the present value of the return on one unit of new capital is greater than or equal to the current tax rate on capital. In this case we assume the investor pays the full tax rate on capital inputs. Suppose, on the other hand, that

$$\frac{P_{K2}}{1+r_1} < t_{K1} \qquad \text{(E16.5)}$$

Here the discounted rate of return on capital is less than the tax rate, and the firm will attempt to reduce its tax payments by moving into the underground economy. The extent to which the firm goes into the underground economy is determined by the gap between the tax rate and the rate of return on investment. That is, the firm pays a tax rate of $\bar{t}_{K1}$ where

$$
\bar{t}_{K1} = t_{K1} \left[1 - \left(\frac{t_{K1} - \dfrac{P_{K2}}{1 + r_2}}{t_{K1}} \right)^{\alpha} \right]
\tag{E16.6}
$$

Here $0 \leq \alpha$ and higher values of α lead to lower values of taxes actually paid. That is, the ratio $\dfrac{\bar{t}_{K1}}{t_{K1}}$ reflects the share of the sector that operates in the formal economy. Hence α represents a firm-specific behavioral variable. An "honest" firm would set $\alpha = 0$, while a firm that is prone to evasion would have a high value for α.[13]

If a sector can avoid paying taxes, as shown previously, by going into the underground economy, why does it pay taxes at all? That is, why does it simply not set $\bar{t}_{K1} = 0$? In the next section we develop a simple approach that supposes that a firm's refusal to pay taxes reduces its ability to borrow from the commercial banking system. Thus, a firm's desire to invest will constrain its evasion of tax payments.

16.3.2   Banking

The banking sector in our model is quite simple and is meant to capture some of the key features and problems in many developing countries. We will suppose that there is one bank for each nonagricultural sector of the economy. There are five such sectors, and hence five banks, corresponding to each of the sectors in the aggregate national income accounts. Such sectoral specialization of the banking system reflects the reality of many developing countries.

We contend that the underground economy affects different sectors in a nonuniform way. Indeed, tax evasion in one sector may benefit the sector at a micro level but may be harmful to the macro economy. Tax evasion varies across sectors not only because of the behavior of firms in that sector but also because different banks could have varying attitudes towards lending to clients who have evaded taxes.

Each bank lends primarily to the sector with which it is associated. The banks are, however, not fully specialized in the sector they correspond to. We make the simplifying assumption that each bank holds a fixed share of the outstanding debt of its particular sector. It then holds additional fixed shares of the debt of each of the remaining sectors. We make this assumption of diversification of assets in order to allow for a situation in which a firm that evades taxes, and thereby enters the underground economy, might receive varying degrees of credit rationing from the different banks to which it applies for loans.

We choose a simple approach to determine the degree of credit rationing that firms face. Our premise is that banks have no direct way of knowing whether specific firms operate in the underground economy. We assume that banks only care about the amount of capital that they estimate the firm may have. If the firm defaults on its loan, then this represents the best estimate of the amount that the bank could seize. The bank would, presumably, be willing to lend an amount equal to at least the estimated value of firm capital. If the firm requests a loan larger than its estimated capital, the bank may choose to grant the full loan, or it may choose to restrict the loan amount. This restriction would depend, in turn, upon the bank's degree of risk aversion.

How can the bank estimate the value of the firm's capital, if this information is not directly revealed by the firm? We assume the borrower is required to show the bank his tax returns in order to obtain a loan. There is a single, flat corporate tax rate, t_{K1}, that the borrowing firm faces. Hence, suppose that T_{K1} represents taxes actually paid by the borrower in period 1. This is known to the bank as the potential borrower is required to present his tax returns. Thus, if the borrower fully complied with his tax obligation and hence carried out no underground activity, the value of his capital, $\hat{K}_1$, would be given by the following:

$$\hat{K}_1 = \frac{T_{K1}}{t_{K1}} \tag{E16.7}$$

Accordingly, the bank would be willing to lend at least $\hat{K}_1$ to the borrower as this would represent a minimum estimate of the value of the firm's capital, which could be seized in the event of a default.[14] Suppose, however, that the amount the firm wishes to borrow, C_{H1}, as in equation (E16.2), such that

$$C_{H1} > \hat{K}_1 \tag{E16.8}$$

In this case the bank lends an amount L_1, where $\widehat{K}_1 \leq L_1 < C_{H1}$, as the bank would not be able to seize the full value of the loan in the case of a default. The situation we have described would, in the case of perfect certainty, have credit rationing when the estimated value of the firm's capital is less than its loan request. If the firm's capital is greater than its loan request, there would be no credit rationing.

In a more realistic case of uncertainty about both the true value of the firm, as well as about the bank's own ability to seize the firm, one might expect the lending process to be somewhat different. Accordingly, we will suppose that a simple functional form determines bank lending as a function of the amount requested as well as the estimated value of the firm's capital. We define the amount the bank lends, L_1, as follows:

$$L_1 = C_{H1} \left[\frac{\dfrac{\widehat{K}_1}{C_{H1}}}{1 + \dfrac{\widehat{K}_1}{C_{H1}}} \right]^{\gamma} = C_{H1} \left[\frac{\widehat{K}_1}{C_{H1+\widehat{K}_1}} \right]^{\gamma} \tag{E16.9}$$

Here γ represents a measure of risk aversion by the bank. If $\gamma = 0$, there are no credit restrictions, and the bank ignores estimates of the borrower's assessed net worth. As γ rises, the bank increasingly restricts lending if the term in brackets is less than 1. If the firm pays no taxes, hence operating entirely in the underground economy, $\hat{K}_1 = 0$ and hence $L_1 = 0$, that is, there is no lending. If $\dfrac{\hat{K}_1}{C_{H1}}$ increases, as would be the case if the value of the firm increases relative to its borrowing request, then $L_1 \Rightarrow C_{H1}$, that is, the bank lends the full value of the request.

Thus, if a firm operates entirely in the underground economy, it will not be able to borrow to finance investment. If banks are highly risk averse, they will never lend more than a firm's estimated net worth, which is based on its tax return. This tax return therefore represents all the information the bank needs in order to determine its response to a request for a loan.

The modeling of consumption remains essentially the same as in our previous modeling of the intertemporal optimizing consumer. Similarly, the government and the foreign sector remain unchanged from before. This reflects our view that corporate tax evasion in developing countries happens between optimizing firms and banks, with relatively little interference from the government. That is, the government does not adjust taxes or expenditures to compensate for tax evasion. Also, there is no significant enforcement or penalties for tax evasion. Intuitively, firms pay the corporate income tax, if only partially, in order to qualify for bank loans that they need to finance investment.

Let us now turn to a numerical implantation of out model.

16.4   Simulations

In this section we carry out simulations designed to give some qualitative notion of the implications for the economy of tax evasion and entry into the underground economy. We use data from Pakistan, but this should be viewed as having only a tenuous relationship to the economy of that country (see Feltenstein and Shah (1993)).[15] We first consider a baseline scenario and then carry out certain counterfactual exercises designed to analyze the effects of alternative tax policies in reducing the size of the underground economy.

In order to use our model for counterfactual simulations, we first generate an equilibrium using benchmark policy parameters. We run the macroeconomic model forward for eight years,[16] giving tax rates and public expenditures their estimated values. In particular, we assume an effective corporate tax rate of 13 percent. We also suppose that the central bank maintains a fixed exchange rate, with the rate being fixed at the level of the first year.

Table 16.2 shows the results of the benchmark simulation. It may be worth making a few remarks concerning the simulated values. We do not wish to make comparisons with actual historical data, given the illustrative nature of this example. First, notice that our model generates moderate rates of growth in real GDP for the first seven periods, after which real growth stagnates. This is primarily the result of the fixed nominal exchange rate, which becomes progressively overvalued. The budget deficit improves and then fluctuates as activity in the underground economy declines. At the same time, however, credit rationing fluctuates. Similarly, interest rates decline and then begin to rise.

It is useful to observe the change in participation of the different sectors in the underground economy. We see that sectors 2 and 3 both have a share of their activity in the underground economy during the initial periods. Over time, their underground activity falls as a share of their total output. The reason for this decline is that the rate of return on capital slowly rises over time, as real GDP rises more rapidly than does investment. However, the rate of change in investment is not uniform across sectors, so underground activity in sector 2 falls more rapidly than in sector 3. We thus see that underground activity may be cyclical.

Suppose now that the government moves to a high tax regime. That is, the government increases the capital tax rate from its current 13 percent to 23 percent. Obviously, this is an arbitrary change but could be viewed as a typical instrument for reducing the budget deficit. Table 16.3 shows the outcomes of this exercise. As might be expected, the increase in the corporate tax rate has a deflationary impact upon the economy. In addition, there is a decline in real GDP, primarily due to the decline in investment in all sectors, as can be seen from a comparison of the final capital stock in all sectors in Tables 16.2 and 16.3.

Table 16.2 Base case

Period	1	2	3	4	5	6	7	8
Nominal GDP 1/	100.0	116.9	106.1	125.1	142.9	159.1	197.5	234.5
Real GDP 1/	100.0	108.4	103.9	105.7	112.9	112.1	119.9	119.4
Price level	100.0	107.8	102.1	118.4	126.6	141.4	164.8	196.7
Interest rate	11.0	0.5	10.9	2.7	11.7	11.5	14.4	16.5
Budget deficit 2/	−6.0	−6.3	0.2	−4.8	1.7	−3.5	0.6	−4.6
Trade balance 2/	−7.6	−7.4	−8.9	−8.3	−9.7	−8.6	−10.9	−10.7

	Net capital stock at end of period 8 1/	Percent of sector in underground economy (Period)				K/C 3/(Period)			Credit granted (Percent) 4/(Period)			
		2	4	6	8	4	6	8	2	4	6	8
Sector 1	100.0	0.0	0.0	0.0	0.0	0.5	5.9	0.9	3.2	100.0	35.0	85.7	47.3
Sector 2	100.0	12.6	0.6	0.0	0.0	11.8	18.0	21.7	30.0	100.0	92.2	94.7	95.6
Sector 3	100.0	20.9	13.3	17.7	10.9	2.1	3.9	4.1	5.7	100.0	67.3	79.7	80.3
Sector 4	100.0	0.0	0.0	0.0	0.0	7.4	12.0	14.1	14.2	100.0	88.3	92.3	93.3
Sector 5	100.0	0.0	0.0	0.0	0.0	1.6	5.5	4.8	5.8	100.0	62.3	84.7	82.7

1/ Normalized to period 1 of the base case.
2/ As a percent of GDP.
3/ Ratio of estimated value of firm's capital to the value of its loan request (as in eq. 4).
4/ Percentage of requested financing that is actually granted to the firm.

Table 16.3 Capital tax rate increase

Period	1	2	3	4	5	6	7	8
Nominal GDP 1/	100.5	117.0	105.5	123.8	128.2	144.2	172.2	200.9
Real GDP 1/	100.5	108.7	103.9	105.1	110.7	110.8	117.4	116.8
Price level	99.9	107.6	101.5	117.8	115.8	130.2	146.7	172.1
Interest rate	11.0	0.4	8.8	−0.4	13.5	12.2	13.4	14.1
Budget deficit 2/	−5.4	−6.2	0.9	−4.4	2.3	−3.6	2.0	−3.8
Trade balance 2/	−7.8	−7.4	−9.0	−8.4	−8.9	−7.9	−10.0	−9.7

Net capital stock at end of period 8 1/	Percent of sector in underground economy (Period)				K/C 3/ (Period)				Credit granted (Percent) 4/ (Period)			
	2	4	6	8	2	4	6	8	2	4	6	8
Sector 1	98.2	64.4	58.9	56.4	23.3	0.2	12.8	0.4	9.3	100.0	18.3	92.7	26.3
Sector 2	98.6	79.1	77.8	75.4	71.2	5.6	10.2	10.7	13.6	100.0	85.4	91.1	91.4
Sector 3	91.2	85.3	85.7	87.4	80.0	0.8	3.4	1.6	3.1	100.0	39.6	77.0	62.0
Sector 4	96.6	61.4	63.1	63.0	48.0	3.2	6.4	6.3	8.4	100.0	76.3	86.7	86.3
Sector 5	97.9	0.0	0.0	0.0	0.0	1.4	5.0	4.3	5.2	100.0	58.7	83.3	81.3

1/ Normalized to period 1 of the base case.
2/ As a percent of GDP.
3/ Ratio of estimated value of firm's capital to the value of its loan request (as in eq. 4).
4/ Percentage of requested financing that is actually granted to the firm.

There are, however, certain unexpected outcomes in this simulation. We see that, with the exception of sector 5, all sectors move partially into the underground economy. They gradually move back into the formal economy as the corresponding investment stagnation, caused partially by credit rationing, results in a higher return on new capital.[17] Since sectors 1–4 are evading taxes, they are also having their credit restricted, as compared to Table 16.2.

Hence, raising the corporate income tax rate has negative consequences beyond those that one might normally expect. The entry of firms into the underground economy leads to a decline in the tax base so that there is only a modest improvement in the budgetary situation. At the same time, credit has been rationed to the non-tax-paying firms, leading to reductions in investment. Thus, the tax increase appears to lead to few benefits.

Suppose now that the government decides to move in the opposite direction. That is, it lowers taxes. Such a policy might be carried out as an attempt to create something like a Laffer effect that increases tax revenues by increasing economic activity in response to lower taxes, while reducing the attractiveness of entry into the underground economy. As an extreme example, we will reduce the corporate income tax rate to 3 percent, from the 13 percent in the base case. Clearly the intent of such a policy would be to stimulate growth by increasing both investment and consumption. At the same time, lower tax rates would presumably discourage

Table 16.4 Capital tax rate decrease

Period	1	2	3	4	5	6	7	8
Nominal GDP 1/	103.7	117.2	120.5	130.4	184.1	219.5	248.2	306.9
Real GDP 1/	101.4	108.0	107.1	106.7	117.7	118.2	123.4	122.5
Price level	102.2	108.6	112.5	122.3	156.4	185.7	201.1	250.5
Interest rate	11.2	2.8	11.7	11.1	15.2	17.6	26.5	38.0
Budget deficit 2/	−7.4	−8.2	−2.2	−7.6	−1.7	−5.9	−5.2	−11.3
Trade balance 2/	−8.0	−7.3	−9.5	−7.9	−10.8	−10.8	−12.0	−12.4

Net capital stock at end of period 8 1/		Percent of sector in underground economy (Period)				K/C 3/ (Period)				Credit granted (Percent) 4/ (Period)			
		2	4	6	8	2	4	6	8	2	4	6	8
Sector 1	104.3	0.0	0.0	0.0	0.0	1.1	5.4	1.6	3.7	100.0	51.7	86.3	61.7
Sector 2	100.0	0.0	0.0	0.0	0.0	38.7	51.3	78.6	90.9	100.0	97.5	98.1	98.7
Sector 3	108.5	0.0	0.0	0.0	0.0	6.1	11.2	10.7	14.3	100.0	85.7	91.7	91.3
Sector 4	102.7	0.0	0.0	0.0	0.0	14.0	22.7	22.7	30.2	100.0	93.3	95.7	95.8
Sector 5	104.8	0.0	0.0	0.0	0.0	3.0	8.3	7.2	10.9	100.0	75.3	89.3	87.3

1/ Normalized to period 1 of the base case.
2/ As a percent of GDP.
3/ Ratio of estimated value of firm's capital to the value of its loan request (as in eq. 4).
4/ Percentage of requested financing that is actually granted to the firm.

underground activity and therefore enhance the tax base. Table 16.4 gives the outcomes of the case with reduced tax rate.

Again, there are some unexpected changes, as compared to the base case. We see that, although there is no underground activity, the rate of capital formation has increased significantly in only one sector. This is largely due to the fact that the budget deficit has more than doubled, leading to crowding out of private investment by public borrowing. There is a corresponding rapid rise in the interest rate, which tends to outweigh the impact on investment than the tax decrease. Indeed, the rate of investment has slowed significantly by the final period. At the same time, the average annual inflation rate rises from 10.1 percent to 13.7 percent. Also, the trade balance deteriorates as increases in the monetary base combine with the assumed fixed exchange rate regime. As might be expected, the share of credit requested that is actually granted has risen, as compared to Table 16.2. As firms fully pay their taxes, the corresponding bank estimate of their net worth rises, leading to lower credit restrictions.

Hence, we may conclude that the low tax regime is not sustainable over time due to increases in the budget and trade deficits, even though it eliminates underground economic activity and reduces credit rationing. Accordingly, we may conclude that it might well be possible to have tax rates that induce some underground behavior yet are nonetheless optimal for the overall economy. At the same time, moderate tax increases can lead to entry into the underground economy and credit rationing that have a significant recessionary impact on the economy.

Notes

1 Feltenstein et al. (2022).
2 As in Braun and Loayza (1993), the underground economy is defined as a set of economic units which do not comply with one or more government-imposed taxes and regulations but whose production is considered legal. See Emran and Stiglitz (2005) for a more general public finance approach to developing countries. See Matovu (2012) for an application to an African country, Uganda.
3 This chapter is based on Dabla-Norris, E., A. Feltenstein. 2005. The Underground Economy and Its Macroeconomic Consequences. *Journal of Policy Reform*, 8 (2), 153–174.
4 In their study of private manufacturing firms in transition countries, Johnson et al. (1997) find that the availability of loans from the banking system was greater in Eastern European countries with small underground economies, such as Poland, than in countries with large hidden activity, such as Ukraine and Russia.
5 Burgess and Stern (1993) note that in developing countries, corporate income taxes represent 17.8 percent of total tax revenues as opposed to 7.6 percent in industrialized countries.
6 Straub (2003) develops a partial equilibrium model of firm's choice between formality and informality with dual credit markets, credit rationing, and a cost of entry into formality. Our paper examines the interaction between the decision to operate formally and the availability of formal credit in a general equilibrium setting and considers the effect on growth.
7 Huq and Sultan (1991) note that in Bangladesh, while borrowing rates from commercial banks were around 12 percent, firms dependent on noninstitutional sources to meet their financing needs paid rates between 48 to 100 percent. McMillan and Woodruff (1999) examine the role informal relationships such as trade credits rather than banks play in meeting financing needs of firms in Vietnam. However, they do not examine the links between informal trading relationships and underground activity.
8 We could have any number of capital types without affecting the structure of the model.
9 We assume that the labor market is not segmented, and there is no wage differential between workers in the underground and the formal economy.
10 We assume that all foreign borrowing for investment is carried out by the government, so that, implicitly, the government is borrowing for the private investor, but the debt incurred is publicly guaranteed.
11 In reality, we can regard the tax rate on capital as the generalized tax rate, including taxation, regulation, and corruption (bribes).
12 Clearly this is an ad hoc assumption. We wish to capture the notion that the decision whether or not to pay taxes is based on the relationship between the return on investment and the tax rate on capital.
13 Here could be a function of the enforcement technology. In our model, however, we assume that there is no enforcement technology or means to enforce tax compliance.
14 We have not explicitly incorporated bankruptcies and defaults in this model, for the sake of simplicity. However, bankruptcies and corresponding bank contractions can be introduced as in Ball and Feltenstein (2001) and Blejer et al. (2002).
15 We have used various parameters derived from Iqbal and Ghulam (1998) as well as Feltenstein and Shah (1993) in order to implement the functional forms of our model.
16 In practice, we take 1993 as the base year. By this we mean that initial allocations of factors and financial assets are given by stocks at the end of 1992. We have data for fiscal and other policy parameters for the next eight years, that is, through 2000.
17 If we compare credit granted in Tables 16.2 and 16.3, we see that the percentage of requested loans that is actually granted generally declines in Table16.3.

References

Abrell, J. 2011. *Transport under Emission Trading: A Computable General Equilibrium Assessment.* Suedwestdeutscher Verlag fuer Hochschulschriften.

Allingham, M. G., A. Sandmo. 1972. Income Tax Evasion: A Theoretical Analysis. *Journal of Public Economics*, 1, 323–338.

Amir, H. 2012. *Tax Policy, Growth, and Income Distribution in Indonesia: A Computable General Equilibrium Analysis.* LAP Lambert Academic Publishing.

André, F. J., M. A. Cardenete, C. Romero. 2010. *Designing Public Policies: An Approach Based on Multi-Criteria Analysis and Computable General Equilibrium Modeling.* Springer.

Auerbach, A., L. Kotlikoff. 1987. Evaluating Fiscal Policy with a Dynamic Simulation Model. *American Economic Review*, 77.

Ball, S., A. Feltenstein. 2001. Bank Failures and Fiscal Austerity: Policy Prescriptions for a Developing Country. *Journal of Public Economics*, 82 (2), 247–270.

Barun Deb Pal, B. D., V. P. Ojha, S. Pohit, J. Roy. 2015. *GHG Emissions and Economic Growth: A Computable General Equilibrium Model Based Analysis for India.* Springer.

Bezanson, J., A. Edelman, S. Karpinski, V. B. Shah. 2017. Julia: A Fresh Approach to Numerical Computing. *SIAM Review*, 59, 65–98.

Blejer, M. I., E. V. Feldman, A. Feltenstein. 2002. Exogenous Shocks, Contagion, and Bank Soundness: A Macroeconomic Framework. *Journal of International Money and Finance*, 21 (1), 33–52.

Bovenberg, A. L., L. H. Goulder. 1996. Optimal Environmental Taxation in the Presence of Other Taxes: General- Equilibrium Analysis. *American Economic Review*, 86 (4), 985–1000.

Braun, J., N. Loayza. 1993. *Taxation, Public Services, and the Informal Sector in a Model of Endogenous Growth.* Unpublished, Harvard University.

Breisinger, C. 2006. *Modelling Infrastructure Investments, Growth and Poverty Impact: A Two-Region Computable General Equilibrium Perspective on Vietnam (Development Economics and Policy).* Peter Lang GmbH, Internationaler Verlag der Wissenschaften.

Brooke, A., D. Kendrick, A. Meeraus. 1992. *GAMS: Release 2.25: A Users Guide.* Scientific Press Series. Boyd and Fraser Publishing Co. <www.gams.com>

Brouwer, L. E. J. 1952. An Intuitionist's Correction of the Fixed-Point Theorem on the Sphere. *Proceedings of the Royal Society, London*, A213, 1–2.

Burfisher, M. E. 2001. *Introduction to Computable General Equilibrium Models.* Cambridge University Press. 3rd Edition.

Burgess, R., N. Stern. 1993. Taxation and Development. *Journal of Economic Literature*, 31 (2), 762–830.

Bye, B., S. Birger, T. Åvitsland. 2003. *Welfare Effects of Vat Reforms: A General Equilibrium Analysis*. Statistisk Sentralbyrå.

Cagan, P. 1956. The Monetary Dynamics of Hyperinflation. In *Studies in the Quantity Theory of Money*, ed. M. Friedman. University of Chicago Press.

Cardenete, M. A., A. Guerra, F. Sancho. 2017. *Applied General Equilibrium: An Introduction*. Springer. 2nd Edition.

Castellanos, K. A. 2021. *Essays in Environmental Economics and International Trade*. Dissertation, Georgia State University.

Castellanos, K. A., G. Heutel. 2019. *Unemployment, Labor Mobility, and Climate Policy*. National Bureau of Economic Research.

Chang, G. H. 2022. *Theory and Programming of Computable General Equilibrium (CGE) Models: A Textbook for Beginners*. World Scientific.

Dabla-Norris, E., A. Feltenstein. 2005. The Underground Economy and Its Macroeconomic Consequences. *Journal of Policy Reform*, 8 (2), 153–174.

Das, K., P. Chakraborti. 2014. *Strategic Trade, Energy Consumption and Welfare: A Computable General Equilibrium Analysis for India*. LAP Lambert Academic Publishing.

Debowicz, D., P. Dorosh, H. Haider, S. Robinson. 2013. A Disaggregated and Macro-Consistent Social Accounting Matrix for Pakistan. *Journal of Economic Structures*, 2, 4. <http://dx.doi.org/10.1186/2193-2409-2-4>

Debreu, G. 1959. *Theory of Value*. Cowles Foundation Monograph. Yale University.

Dervis, K., J. De Melo, S. Robinson. 1981. A General Equilibrium Analysis of Foreign Exchange Shortages in a Developing Economy. *The Economic Journal*, 91 (364), 891–906.

Dervis, K., J. De Melo, S. Robinson. 1982. *General Equilibrium Models for Development Policy*. Cambridge University Press.

De Soto, H. 1989. *The Other Path*. Harper and Row.

Dixon, P. B., M. Jerie, M. T. Rimmer. 2018. *Trade Theory in Computable General Equilibrium Models: Armington, Krugman and Melitz*. Springer. 1st Edition.

Dixon, P. B., D. Jorgenson (Eds.). 2012. *Handbook of Computable General Equilibrium Modeling (Volumes: 1A and 1B) (Handbooks in Economics)*. North Holland. 1st Edition.

Do, X. 2009. *Apply Computable General Equilibrium (CGE) Model*. VDM Verlag.

Doi, M. 2003. *Computable General Equilibrium Approaches in Urban and Regional Policy Studies*. WSPC. Illustrated Edition.

Emran, M. S., J. E. Stiglitz. 2005. On Selective Indirect Tax Reform in Developing Countries. *Journal of Public Economics*, 89, 599–623.

Eromenko, I. 2011. *Accession to the WTO: Computable General Equilibrium Analysis: The Case of Ukraine*. LAP Lambert Academic Publishing.

Fair, R. C. 1984. *Specification, Estimation, and Analysis of Macroeconomic Models*. Harvard University Press.

Fehr, H., C. Rosenberg, W. Wiegard. 1995. *Welfare Effects of Value-Added Tax Harmonization in Europe: A Computable General Equilibrium Analysis*. Springer.

Feltenstein, A. 1997. An Analysis of the Implications for the Gold Mining Industry of Alternative Tax Policies: A Regional Disaggregated Model for Australia. *Economic Record*, 73 (223), 305–314.

Feltenstein, A., J. Martinez-Vazquez, B. Datta, S. Fatehin. 2022. A General Equilibrium Model of Value Added Tax Evasion: An Application to Pakistan. *International Economics and Economic Policy*, 19 (3), 537–556.

Feltenstein, A., C. Mejia, D. Newhouse, G. Sedrakyan. 2017. The Poverty Implications of Alternative Tax Reforms: Results from a Numerical Application to Pakistan. *Journal of Asian Economics*, 52, 12–31.

Feltenstein, A., S. Morris. 1990. Fiscal Stabilization and Exchange Rate Instability: A Theoretical Approach and Some Policy Conclusions using Mexican Data. *Journal of Public Economics*, 42, 329–356.

Feltenstein, A., A. Shah. 1993. General Equilibrium Effects of Taxation on Investment in a Developing Country: The Case of Pakistan. *Public Finance*, 48 (3), 366–386.

Feltenstein, A., F. Plassmann. 2008. The Welfare Analysis of a Free Trade Zone: Intermediate Goods and the Asian Tigers. *World Economy*, 905–924.

Feltenstein, A., M. Shamloo. 2013. Tax Reform, the Informal Economy, and Bank Financing of Capital Formation. *International Tax and Public Finance*, 20 (1), 1–28.

Fossati, A., W. Wiegard (Eds.). 2002. *Policy Evaluation with Computable General Equilibrium Models*. Routledge. 1st Edition.

Fullerton, D., A. T. King, J. B. Shoven, J. Whalley. 1981. Corporate Tax Integration in the United States: A General Equilibrium Approach. *American Economic Review*, 71, 677–691.

Gilbert, J., H. Beladi, K. Choi (Eds.). 2010. *New Developments in Computable General Equilibrium Analysis for Trade Policy (Frontiers of Economics and Globalization)*. Emerald Publishing Limited. Illustrated Edition.

Ginsburgh, V., M. Keyzer. 1997. *The Structure of Applied General Equilibrium Models*. MIT Press.

Gordon, R., W. Li. 2009. Tax Structures in Developing Countries: Many Puzzles and a Possible Explanation. *Journal of Public Economics*, 93, 855–866.

Harberger, A. C. 1962. The Incidence of the Corporation Income Tax. *Journal of Political Economy*, 70 (3), 215–240.

Harrison, G. W., T. F. Rutherford, D. G. Tarr. 1997. Quantifying the Uruguay Round. *Economic Journal*, 107, 1405–1430.

Hayek, F. A von. 1935. *Collectivist Economic Planning – Critical Studies on the Possibilities of Socialism*, ed. with an intro. and a concluding essay by F. A von Hayek. Routledge & Kegan Paul.

Hayek, F. A von. 1940. Socialist Calculation: The Competitive 'Solution'. *Economica*, 7 (26), 125–149.

Hosoe, N., K. Gasawa, H. Hashimoto. 2010. *Textbook of Computable General Equilibrium Modeling: Programming and Simulations*. Palgrave Macmillan.

Huq, M., M. Sultan. 1991. Informality' in Development: The Poor as Entrepreneurs in Bangladesh. In *The Silent Revolution*, ed. A. Chickering, M. Salahdine. International Center for Economic Growth.

Iqbal, Z., M. Z. Ghulam. 1998. Macroeconomic Determinants of Economic Growth in Pakistan. *The Pakistan Development Review*, 37 (2), 125–148.

Johnson, S., D. Kaufmann, A. Shleifer. 1997. *The Unofficial Economy in Transition*. Brookings Paper on Economic Activity, Brookings Institute, 159–239.

Kabir, K., H. Dudu. 2020. *Using Computable General Equilibrium Models to Analyze Economic Benefits of Gender-Inclusive Policies*. MTI Practice Notes. World Bank.

Kehoe, P. J., T. J. Kehoe. 1995. A Primer on Static Applied General Equilibrium Models. In *Modeling North American Economic Integration*, ed. P. J. Kehoe, T. J. Kehoe. Kluwer Academic Publishers, 1–31.

Kiyotaki, N., J. Moore. 1997. Credit Cycles. *Journal of Political Economy*, 105 (2), 211–248.

Koopmans, T. C. 1957. *Three Essays on the State of Economic Science*. McGraw-Hill.

Kuhn, H. W. 1960. Some Combinatorial Lemmas in Topology. *IBM Journal of Research and Development*, 5, 518–524.

Kydland, F., E. Prescott. 1977. Rules Rather Than Discretion: The Inconsistency of Optimal Plans. *Journal of Political Economy*, 85 (3), 473–491.

Lange, O. 1967. The Computer and the Market. In *Socialism, Capitalism and Economic Growth – Essays Presented to Maurice Dobb*, ed. C. H. Feinstein. Cambridge University Press, 158–161.

Lemke, C. E., J. T. Howson. 1964. Equilibrium Points of Bimatrix Games. *Journal of the Society for Individual and Applied Mathematics*, 12, 413–423.

Madden, J. R., H. Shibusawa, Y. Higano (Eds.). 2020. *Environmental Economics and Computable General Equilibrium Analysis: Essays in Memory of Yuzuru Miyata*. Springer.

Mainar-Causapé, A. J., E. Ferrari, S. McDonald. 2018. *Social Accounting Matrices: Basic Aspects and Main Steps for Estimation*. European Commission, JRC Technical Report.

Matovu, J. 2012. Trade Reforms and Horizontal Inequalities: The Case of Uganda. *European Journal of Development Research*, 24 (5), 753–776.

McMillan, J., C. Woodruff. 1999. Interfirm Relationships and Informal Credit in Vietnam. *The Quarterly Journal of Economics*, 114 (4), 1285–1320.

Meng, S., M. Siriwardana. 2017. *Assessing the Economic Impact of Tourism: A Computable General Equilibrium Modelling Approach*. Palgrave Macmillan. 1st Edition.

Merrill, H. O. 1972. *Application and Extension of an Algorithm that Computes Fixed Points of Certain Upper Semi-Continuous Point to Set Mappings*. Ph.D. Thesis, Department of Industrial Engineering, University of Michigan.

Miller, M. H., J. E. Spencer. 1977. The Static Economic Effects of the UK Joining the EEC: A General Equilibrium Approach. *The Review of Economic Studies*, 44 (1), 71–93.

Mohammed, T., N. Jabin. 2019. *A Computable General Equilibrium Analysis: For Estimating A Cost Effective of Climate Change Adaptation Policy for Malaysia*. LAP Lambert Academic Publishing.

Park, I. 1995. *Regional Integration Among the ASEAN Nations: A Computable General Equilibrium Model Study*. Praeger. Illustrated Edition.

Perali, F., P. L. Scandizzo (Eds.). 2018. *The New Generation of Computable General Equilibrium Models: Modeling the Economy*. Springer.

Pyatt, G., J. I. Round (Eds.). 1985. *Social Accounting Matrices: A Basis for Planning*. World Bank.

Radulescu, D., M. Stimmelmayr. 2010. The Impact of the 2008 German Corporate Tax Reform: A Dynamic CGE Analysis. *Economic Modelling*, 27 (1), 454–467.

Reinert, K. A., D. W. Roland-Holst. 1997. Social Accounting Matrices. In *Applied Methods for Trade Policy Analysis: A Handbook*, ed. J. F. Francois, K. A. Reinert. Cambridge University Press.

Robbins, L. 1937. *Economic Planning and International Order*. Palgrave Macmillan.

Scarf, H.E. 1967a. The Approximation of Fixed Points of a Continuous Mapping. *SIAM Journal of Applied Mathematics*, 15, 1328–1343.

Scarf, H. E. 1967b. The Core of N Person Game. *Econometrica: Journal of the Econometric Society*, 35 (1), 50–69.

Scarf, H. E. 1973. *The Computation of Economic Equilibria*. Cowles Foundation Monograph 24.

Schneider, F., D. H. Enste. 2000. Shadow Economies: Size, Causes, and Consequences. *Journal of Economic Literature*, 38 (1), 77–114.

Selvanathan, S., E. A. Selvanathan. 1998. *An Econometric Study of Gold Production and Prices*. Department of Economics, University of Western Australia, Discussion Paper 98.02.

Shleifer, A., R. W. Vishny. 1993. Corruption. *The Quarterly Journal of Economics*, 108 (3), 599–617.

Shoven, J. B. 1974. A Proof of the Existence of a General Equilibrium with Ad Valorem Commodity Taxes. *Journal of Economic Theory*, 8, 1–25.

Shoven, J. B., J. Whalley. 1972. A General Equilibrium Calculation of the Effects of Differential Taxation of Income from Capital in the U.S. *Journal of Public Economics*, 1 (3–4), 281–321.

Shoven, J., J. Whalley. 1973. General Equilibrium with Taxes: A Computational Procedure and an Existence Proof. *The Review of Economic Studies*, 40 (4), 475–489.

Shoven, J., J. Whalley. 1992. *Applying General Equilibrium*. Cambridge University Press.

Smith, A. 2003. *The Wealth of the Nations*. Bantam (Original work published 1776).

Straub, S. 2003. *Informal Sector: The Credit Market Channel*. Department of Economics Working Paper. University of Edinburgh.

Strotz, R. 1956. Myopia and Inconsistency in Dynamic Utility Maximization. *Review of Economic Studies*, 23 (3), 165–180.

Tanaka, T., N. Hosoe, H. Qiu. 2012. *Risk Assessment of Food Supply: A Computable General Equilibrium Approach*. Cambridge Scholars Publishing. Unabridged edition.

Tanzi, V. 2001. Uses and Abuses of Estimates of the Underground Economy. *The Economic Journal*, 109 (456), 338–347.

Tanzi, V., L. Schuknecht. 2000. *Public Spending in the 20th Century: A Global Perspective*. Cambridge University Press.

Taylor, L. (Ed.). 1990. *Socially Relevant Policy Analysis: Structuralist Computable General Equilibrium Models for the Developing World*. MIT Press.

Varian, H. 1974. A Third Remark on the Number of Equilibria of an Economy. *Econometrica*, 43, 985–986.

Walras, L. 1954. *Elements of Pure Economics*, trans. W. Jaffe. American Economic Association and Royal Economic Society.

Index

Printed in the United States
by Baker & Taylor Publisher Services